Prescription Drugs

Other Books in the Current Controversies Series

Current
CONTROVERSIES

| Prescription Drugs

Sylvia Engdahl, Book Editor

GREENHAVEN PRESS
A part of Gale, Cengage Learning

GALE
CENGAGE Learning·

Farmington Hills, Mich · San Francisco · New York · Waterville, Maine

Elizabeth Des Chenes, *Director, Content Strategy*
Douglas Dentino, *Manager, New Product*

For more information, contact:
Greenhaven Press
27500 Drake Rd.
Farmington Hills, MI 48331-3535
Or you can visit our Internet site at gale.cengage.com

For product information and technology assistance, contact us at

Gale Customer Support, 1-800-877-4253
For permission to use material from this text or product, submit all requests online at www.cengage.com/permissions

Further permissions questions can be emailed to permissionrequest@cengage.com

Articles in Greenhaven Press anthologies are often edited for length to meet page requirements. In addition, original titles of these works are changed to clearly present the main thesis and to explicitly indicate the author's opinion. Every effort is made to ensure that Greenhaven Press accurately reflects the original intent of the authors. Every effort has been made to trace the owners of copyrighted material.

Cover image copyright © branislapudar/ShutterStock.com.

LIBRARY OF CONGRESS CATALOGING-IN-PUBLICATION DATA

Prescription drugs / Sylvia Engdahl, book editor.
    p. cm. -- (Current controversies)
    Summary: "Current Controversies: Prescription Drugs: This series covers today's most current national and international issues and the most important opinions of the past and present. The purpose of the series is to introduce readers to all sides of contemporary controversies"-- Provided by publisher.
    Includes bibliographical references and index.
    ISBN 978-0-7377-6888-6 (hardback) -- ISBN 978-0-7377-6889-3 (paperback)
    1. Drugs--Juvenile literature. 2. Drug abuse--Prevention--Juvenile literature. I. Engdahl, Sylvia, editor of compilation.
    RM301.17.P74 2014
    615.1--dc23
                                             2013047499

Printed in the United States of America
1 2 3 4 5 6 7 18 17 16 15 14

Contents

Chapter 1: Are People Taking Too Many Unnecessary Prescription Drugs?

Yes: Prescription Drugs Are Promoted for Conditions That Do Not Warrant Them

No: Many People Do Not Take Enough Medication to Protect Their Health

Chapter 2: Are Prescription Drug Prices Unjustifiably High?

Use of prescription drugs often averts the need for more expensive health care, but the expense of drugs is great for the public and insurers. High prices are caused partly by the cost of research and development and by patent protection for new drugs. There is wide variation in different insurance coverage plans. However, the rate of drug price increases is expected to slow down.

Yes: The Prices of Prescription Drugs Are Excessive

In the past few years there has been a large increase in the number of teens who abuse prescription drugs. One in four teens has done so at least once. Many teens say their parents do not mind this as much as they would mind the use of illegal drugs, yet prescription drugs are just as dangerous if they are misused. Parents need to educate their kids about the dangers and set a good example.

Chapter 4: What Other Problems Are Occurring with Prescription Drugs?

The drugs people take pass through the body and enter waste treatment facilities, from which they escape into waterways and are often toxic to wildlife. Contamination of the environment is getting worse and worse because of rapid growth in the consumption of prescription drugs. Many experts now believe that environmental impact should be considered before drugs are approved.

The federal Food and Drug Administration is considering allowing some drugs that formerly required a prescription to be sold without one. People are better informed than they used to be and they want more control over their own health-care decisions, as well as to spend less on medical care. But groups that oppose individual freedom of choice are against such proposals.

Foreword

By definition, controversies are "discussions of questions in which opposing opinions clash" (*Webster's Twentieth Century Dictionary Unabridged*). Few would deny that controversies are a pervasive part of the human condition and exist on virtually every level of human enterprise. Controversies transpire between individuals and among groups, within nations and between nations. Controversies supply the grist necessary for progress by providing challenges and challengers to the status quo. They also create atmospheres where strife and warfare can flourish. A world without controversies would be a peaceful world; but it also would be, by and large, static and prosaic.

The Series' Purpose

The purpose of the Current Controversies series is to explore many of the social, political, and economic controversies dominating the national and international scenes today. Titles selected for inclusion in the series are highly focused and specific. For example, from the larger category of criminal justice, Current Controversies deals with specific topics such as police brutality, gun control, white collar crime, and others. The debates in Current Controversies also are presented in a useful, timeless fashion. Articles and book excerpts included in each title are selected if they contribute valuable, long-range ideas to the overall debate. And wherever possible, current information is enhanced with historical documents and other relevant materials. Thus, while individual titles are current in focus, every effort is made to ensure that they will not become quickly outdated. Books in the Current Controversies series will remain important resources for librarians, teachers, and students for many years.

In addition to keeping the titles focused and specific, great care is taken in the editorial format of each book in the series. Book introductions and chapter prefaces are offered to provide background material for readers. Chapters are organized around several key questions that are answered with diverse opinions representing all points on the political spectrum. Materials in each chapter include opinions in which authors clearly disagree as well as alternative opinions in which authors may agree on a broader issue but disagree on the possible solutions. In this way, the content of each volume in Current Controversies mirrors the mosaic of opinions encountered in society. Readers will quickly realize that there are many viable answers to these complex issues. By questioning each author's conclusions, students and casual readers can begin to develop the critical thinking skills so important to evaluating opinionated material.

Current Controversies is also ideal for controlled research. Each anthology in the series is composed of primary sources taken from a wide gamut of informational categories including periodicals, newspapers, books, US and foreign government documents, and the publications of private and public organizations. Readers will find factual support for reports, debates, and research papers covering all areas of important issues. In addition, an annotated table of contents, an index, a book and periodical bibliography, and a list of organizations to contact are included in each book to expedite further research.

Perhaps more than ever before in history, people are confronted with diverse and contradictory information. During the Persian Gulf War, for example, the public was not only treated to minute-to-minute coverage of the war, it was also inundated with critiques of the coverage and countless analyses of the factors motivating US involvement. Being able to sort through the plethora of opinions accompanying today's major issues, and to draw one's own conclusions, can be a complicated and frustrating struggle. It is the editors' hope that Current Controversies will help readers with this struggle.

Introduction

"Drug companies have succeeded in defining some normal conditions as "diseases" and . . . people have come to believe that every form of distress can and should be overcome by taking drugs."

In recent years there has been a great deal of criticism of pharmaceutical companies. Many people believe that the cost of prescription drugs is much too high, and indeed, paying for medications is a real hardship not only for those with low incomes, but for anyone who is not wealthy—especially the elderly. Prescription drug costs have increased tremendously in the past few decades. Drug companies point out, however, that this is due to the fact that there are now a lot more drugs available for previously untreatable medical problems, and that these drugs are extremely expensive to develop. While it is true that many drugs can be manufactured cheaply, drug prices are not based on just the cost of production; they have to cover the large sums spent on research and testing. It does not seem fair that people who are ill should have to pay more than they can afford for medication, and yet drug companies cannot be expected to sell their products at a loss.

Another issue with prescription drugs is the frequent prescribing of medications to people who are not ill, in the hope of preventing future illness. Whether this practice really does prevent illness is debatable. Moreover, society's perception of "illness" has been expanding. Serious illnesses affect comparatively few people, and the cost of developing drugs for these illnesses far exceeds what could be recovered by selling them, even at high prices. Drug companies can make money only from drugs prescribed to large numbers of people. To increase their revenues, drug manufacturers vigorously promote new

drugs that some observers believe are not needed, either because older, cheaper treatments for the same disease already
exist or because the conditions they are designed to treat are
not really diseases at all.

Two kinds of promotion are causing considerable concern
at present. First, drug companies have a great deal of direct
influence on doctors. As an article in the January 2008 issue
of the *AARP Bulletin* states:

> For years, pharmaceutical companies have courted America's
> doctors with an ever-growing intensity, showering them
> with billions of dollars' worth of gifts, consulting fees, and
> trips to persuade them to prescribe their drugs. But now,
> patient advocates and lawmakers are out to break up those
> relationships, arguing that physicians—working amid the
> clutter of the drug industry's free samples, pens, clipboards,
> calculators and pizza boxes—often lose sight of the patient's
> best interests.

Second, drug companies advertise on television and in
magazines, a practice some consumer advocates feel should be
illegal. Defenders of the practice, however, believe that ban-
ning such ads would be a violation of free speech. These ads
are directed not to people who are being treated for a recog-
nized illness, but to members of the general public who have
not previously believed that their problems required medication. The drug companies view such ads as educational. An
increasing number of commentators view them as attempts to
convince healthy people that they are sick.

A more subtle but even greater way in which the pharmaceutical industry influences the public is through information
provided to the media. Most reporters are not medical experts. They do not intentionally slant what they write, but
they know what makes a good story; glowing accounts of the
potential benefits of a new treatment attract more readers
than disclaimers about side effects, risks, or lack of evidence.
If a drug company's news release omits the latter, it is likely to

be taken at face value. People want to believe in the existence of cures. So do doctors, most of whom are motivated by a genuine desire to help those who consult them. It is not surprising that the idea of a "miracle drug" for every problem has taken hold.

Of course, there are many drugs that do effectively treat illness, and there is real hope that presently incurable diseases can be conquered in the future. But there is a darker side to the glorification of prescription drugs in the public mind. More and more, society is absorbing the view that the solution to all discomfort is chemical. Many observers point out that the drug companies have succeeded in defining some normal conditions as "diseases" and that people have come to believe that every form of distress can and should be overcome by taking drugs. This is an understandable mindset for those who, since childhood, have been medicated whenever they were sick or merely unhappy, sometimes even at the insistence of school authorities. An extension of this attitude is the tendency to turn to illegally obtained drugs—both recreational and prescription—in the hope of feeling better.

Thus, in recent years there has been a tremendous increase in prescription drug abuse, which the Centers for Disease Control and Prevention (CDC) has now classified as an epidemic. The belief that pharmaceuticals are less dangerous than banned drugs such as crack and heroin is a common, though false, belief. In some respects they are even more dangerous because they are more accessible and users do not expect medical drugs to do any serious harm. Yet people who take prescription drugs without having been diagnosed with the condition the drugs were intended to treat are as likely to be harmed—or perhaps even killed—as those who take street drugs. And it happens all too often. Deaths from overdosing on prescription painkillers are on the rise, and users who do not die often need emergency care or incur long-term damage to their bodies. Those affected—either personally or by drug abuse on the part of family members—are of all ages, from teens to parents to older people, and it is considered a major public health problem.

Until recently, it was generally assumed that medications were an unquestionable blessing. In fact, before 1938 there was no such thing as a "prescription drug;" only narcotics required a physician's authorization and prescriptions were written simply as advice. In the seventy-five years since controls were first established, more and more drug-related problems have arisen, many of which are discussed in this book. Like other technologies, pharmaceuticals have brought trouble as well as benefits. Prescription drugs can be of great help to many who need them, but they should always be taken with caution.

CHAPTER 1

Are People Taking Too Many Unnecessary Prescription Drugs?

Chapter Preface

Over the past few decades the use of prescription drugs has risen dramatically. In part, the increase is due to the development of new drugs to treat serious illnesses that could not be effectively treated in the past. This is of unquestionable benefit to the patients stricken by those illnesses. But at the same time, more and more drugs are being given to people with less serious conditions, and that trend is more debatable.

Two main problems are pointed out by experts who oppose such extensive use of prescription drugs. First, they argue, it is not always safe; a recent study estimated that one hundred thousand Americans die each year from prescription drugs taken as directed by their doctors. And second, labeling common human problems "illness" leads people once thought healthy to believe they are sick. According to the Centers for Disease Control and Prevention (CDC) nearly half of Americans use one or more prescription drugs on a regular basis, and in some age groups the percentage is much higher. If half the population suffers from some sort of abnormality requiring medication, the term "normal" has lost all meaning.

Most people assume that drugs approved by the government are guaranteed to be both safe and effective—that they cause serious harm when taken as directed only if there has been negligence on the part of the US Food and Drug Administration (FDA). But it is not as simple as that, for when it comes to drugs, "safe" is a relative term. No drug is 100 percent safe for everyone. All drugs have multiple effects; calling the undesired ones "side" effects does not mean that they are insignificant. And the action of a given drug is different on different people. So the testing of drugs is a matter of evaluating statistics, not of proving that the drug will never affect anybody adversely.

A great deal depends on how the statistics are obtained—the number of people on which the drug is tested, what other drug or placebo it is compared with, and so forth. If the test is not well designed, its results will not be valid, and medical researchers do sometimes fail to consider all the factors that should be allowed for in the design of their experiments. But even the best-designed tests cannot uncover all the adverse effects a drug may have, because these effects may not occur until the drug has been taken by millions of patients. Or they may not show up until it has been used for a longer period of time than any test can last.

So whether a drug should be called safe is not an absolute judgment, and there is controversy about where to draw the line. For instance, how long should testing continue? If the drug is put on the market too quickly, adverse effects—perhaps even fatal ones—may later appear. On the other hand, if its approval is delayed too long, people who could be helped by it may suffer unnecessarily and, in some cases, may die while they are waiting.

Is it worse for a few people to be harmed by a new drug than for many others to be harmed by the lack of it? The answer to this question depends in part on the number of people likely to be affected, but that number cannot be known in advance. Furthermore, few would say that it is acceptable for a drug to do serious damage to some patients, even if far more will be helped by its availability. If damaging effects are known to be rare, some researchers believe that the benefits to the public justify approval and widespread use of the drug. Another question must be asked, however: How serious are those effects, especially when compared to the condition the drug is intended to treat?

It would seem obvious that minor health problems do not warrant the use of dangerous drugs. But not everyone agrees about what problems are minor. For example, many widely promoted drugs, such as those that lower cholesterol, are designed not to cure illness, but to lessen the *statistical* chance of future illness—in other words, to reduce "risk factors" which in themselves have recently been defined as "disease." The individuals who take such drugs might never develop the illnesses they are trying to avoid. Is the attempt at prevention worth the risk of harmful side effects when only a small percentage of those who take such drugs would have later been affected by the disease? That issue is rarely raised; fear that serious illness will strike in the future distracts both doctors and patients from asking whether preventative medication might do more harm than good.

Many observers also feel that it is wrong to prescribe pills—particularly to children—for mere problems in dealing with life, such as hyperactivity, shyness, or depression, that used to be considered natural consequences of being human. When every deviation from an unattainable state of perfection is defined as sickness, it is not surprising that some people react to unhappiness by obtaining prescription drugs illegally in the hope of feeling better. And yet, medication does sometimes help when problems are severe; so it is difficult to determine where it is truly warranted.

Pharmaceutical Companies Push Doctors to Prescribe Unnecessary Drugs

Paul J. Rosch

Paul J. Rosch is chairman of the board of directors of the American Institute of Stress. He is a doctor who has written extensively about the role of stress in health and illness.

Up until the last century, the primary purpose of developing new drugs was to treat or prevent disease. Over the past six decades, there has been a progressive proliferation of pharmaceutical companies promoting multiple medications, many of which fiercely compete for the same patients. As a result, their goal is now to produce patented products to increase income for executives and shareholders, rather than the health of consumers. There is little doubt that this has been phenomenally successful, as evidenced by the fact that drug companies have consistently been the most profitable U.S. industry, and that pharmacracy now dominates the practice of medicine.

Pharmacracy is a term that was coined in 1974 by [psychiatrist] Thomas Szasz because "while we have words to describe medicine as a healing art, we have none to describe it as a method of social control or political rule." It is derived from the Greek *pharmakon* (medicine or drug) and *kratein* (to rule or to control), just as theocracy is rule by religious sects and democracy is rule by the majority of people.

Pharmacracy refers to 1) The transfer of authority for defining diseases and how to treat them from physicians to politicians (and others who are reimbursed by pharmaceutical manufacturers). 2) A deliberate blurring of boundaries between disease and non-disease and between medical treatment of disease and the use of medical personnel or technology to alter non-disease. 3) The severing of contractual economic relationships between doctors who deliver medical care and patients who receive it. While originally designed to illustrate how this applied to the specialty of psychiatry, pharmacracy has now metastasized to permeate and essentially control virtually every facet of medical research and practice.

> *Excess utilization of hospitalization and diagnostic procedures is driven by multiple factors, such as . . . the pervasive belief that newer and/or more expensive drugs and technology are always better.*

This emphasis on disease mongering and the selling of sickness has been facilitated by regulatory agencies, legislators, prestigious medical institutions and organizations, prominent physicians, insurance companies and other influential groups or individuals, all of which receive huge payments and other perks for their promotional efforts. Approximately $5 billion are spent annually on direct to consumer ads on TV and print media presumably designed for educational purposes, but are primarily messages that hype benefits and minimize dangers, which is why they are banned in all other countries save New Zealand. The price tag for up to 100,000 drug company representatives to promote products to U.S. practicing physicians is well over $7 billion/year. The pharmaceutical industry, health organizations and insurance companies spend over $1.5 million/day lobbying members of Congress to preserve and possibly increase their current exorbitant profits. It is estimated that annual pharmaceutical marketing expenses may be close to $57 billion, which is over twice as much as is invested for drug research and development.

Why We Spend Much More on Health Care but Are Sicker and Die Earlier

As a result, the U.S. pays much more for health care per capita than any other country. We spend over 44 percent more than Switzerland, which is the next highest, over twice as much as Great Britain, and four times as much as South Korea, whose citizens live at least a year longer than we do. Several months ago, a *New York Times* article touted a Centers For Disease Control [and Prevention] report indicating that in 2007, Americans were living almost two-and-a-half months longer, nearly 78 years, up from 77.7 the previous year. Not mentioned was the fact that some 22 countries had life expectancies of 80 or higher. . . .

Approximately 250,000 patients die each year from physician related (iatrogenic) activities, which now represent the third leading cause of death. Most of these occur in hospitals but the total is probably much higher, since the vast majority of iatrogenic errors are never reported or not diagnosed.

This excess utilization of hospitalization and diagnostic procedures is driven by multiple factors, such as practicing defensive medicine by doctors trying to avoid lawsuits; unrealistic expectation and demands by patients that result from direct to consumer advertising; the pervasive belief that newer and/or more expensive drugs and technology are always better; and the current reimbursement system that encourages doctors to order tests and perform procedures that may not be necessary, but are reimbursed by insurance companies, Medicare, Medicaid and other fiscal intermediaries since they are easy to justify. The use of sophisticated imaging procedures has steadily increased, and some, such as MRIs [magnetic resonance imaging] and CTT [computerized transaxial tomography] scans, deliver doses of ionizing radiation up to 50 times higher than a routine chest x-ray or mammogram. One study estimated that 29,000 unnecessary deaths from cancer could result from just the CTT scans performed in

2007. The U.S. also has the most MRI machines, 26.5 per million population, compared with 5.6 in the U.K. [United Kingdom]. However, these and other equipment expenses pale in comparison to the costs of maintaining pharmacracy.

How Merck's Fosamax Converted the Worried Well into Paying Patients

In a 1976 *Fortune* magazine interview, Merck CEO Henry Gadsen complained that his only customers were people who were sick, and he wanted his company to make drugs for healthy individuals so he could "sell to everyone." Three decades later, pharmacracy has turned that dream into an expensive and dangerous nightmare. Drug companies have successfully expanded the definition of illness and lowered the criteria for prescribing their products by creating millions of new patients who fear they are sick or will become sick from some trivial or poorly understood ailment. This has been accomplished by a combination of manipulative marketing and massive corruption of the medical care system that has permitted ordinary complaints to become magnified and "medicalized". This triumph of spurious and often specious salesmanship over science has also been responsible for turning healthy people into paying patients by creating new diseases, exaggerating the dangers of relatively insignificant complaints and/or the benefits of drugs to prevent age related but asymptomatic disorders like osteopenia . . . , such medications often produce more damage than the conditions for which they are prescribed.

Osteoporosis refers to a reduction of bone mineral density that may increase the risk for hip, vertebral body, rib and other fractures. Bone density tends to decrease with age, especially in postmenopausal women, due to a decline in the protective effects of estrogen. Other risk factors include rheumatoid arthritis, taking corticosteroids, vitamin D deficiency, a family history of fractures, insufficient exercise, smoking, excess alcohol, and malnutrition. The diagnosis of osteoporosis originally depended on evidence of a spontaneous fracture. In many instances, there were few symptoms, such as vertebral fractures that are common in osteoporotic elderly women and are responsible for loss of height and the "Dowager's Hump." Over 50 years ago, in an attempt to improve the diagnosis of osteoporosis, our Department of Metabolism at Walter Reed [Army Medical Center] published the first definitive article dealing with this. . . .

Over the next several decades, the development of more sophisticated imaging procedures progressively led to improved methods for measuring bone density. Since these advances had the potential for objectively defining osteoporosis, the World Health Organization convened a group of international experts in Rome in 1992 for that specific purpose. It was not an easy assignment, since all bones start to lose density after the age of 30. It was unclear how much loss might fall into a normal range at ages 50, 60, or 70. And how much osteoporosis was necessary to put women at such a significantly increased risk that it should be viewed as a disease? One of the participants, Dr. Anna Tosteson, Professor of Medicine at Dartmouth Medical School, said they spent several days going over research reports in an attempt to decide where on a graph of diminishing bone density with age they should draw a line. "And as I recall, it was very hot in the meeting room, and people were in shirt sleeves and, you know, it was time to kind of move on, if you will. And, I can't quite frankly remember who it was who stood up and drew the picture and said, 'Well, let's just do this.'"

In other words, in order to end the stalemate, someone drew an arbitrary line through the graph, and it was decreed that every women on one side of this line had osteoporosis. But there were other problems and questions, such as "How should you categorize those women who are just on the other side of that line?" They decided "more or less off the cuff" to use the term osteopenia from the Greek *osteon* (bone) and *penia* (poverty). This "bone poverty" osteopenia classification was created solely to assist public health researchers who require clear categories for their studies. In 1994, the World Health Organization experts agreed to define osteoporosis as a bone density 2.5 standard deviations below that of an average 30-year-old white woman. They then defined osteopenia as a bone density one standard deviation below that of an average 30-year-old white woman. Both of these definitions were entirely arbitrary. They were designed to track the emergence of a problem in different populations, not as a measurement that had any precise diagnostic, much less therapeutic, significance for an individual. As Tosteson noted, "It was never imagined that people would come to think of osteopenia as a disease to be treated.". . .

[Osteopenia] is an artificial and completely invented condition that has no symptoms or signs. It is not a disease that requires treatment.

However, Merck saw this as a opportunity to realize its dream of treating healthy and asymptomatic people come true. . . .

1997 was a banner year for Merck. Its bogus Bone Measurement Institute and other interested groups it funded successfully lobbied Congress to pass The Bone Measurement Act, which changed Medicare reimbursement rules to cover all bone density scans. As Steve Cummings, an authority on bone density research noted, "It is impossible to overemphasize just how important this legislation was. Up to that point patients needed to pay for bone densitometry out of their own pocket, but once it's reimbursed, clinicians get paid for making measurements of bone density." Most of the machines that were leased or purchased by doctors as result of this ruling could scan peripheral bone and provide a report with three distinct colors: green (normal), red (osteoporosis) and yellow for osteopenia. Cummings also emphasized "The very existence of the word 'osteopenia' on a medical report, along with the clear green-yellow-red graph, had a profound effect. When millions of women are getting the word 'osteopenia' from the bone density test that they are getting in their 50s and 60s, they get worried. When a clinician sees the word 'osteopenia' on a report, they think that it's a disease. They want to know: What should I do?" Merck had the answer. 1997 was also the year they obtained FDA [US Food and Drug Administration] approval for Fosamax to treat osteopenia, although there were no long-term studies to show any benefits. . . .

Speculations have been transformed into facts in deceptive ads despite the fact that they are not supported (and in many instances have been contradicted) by scientific studies.

Confusing Osteopenia, Osteoporosis, and Bone Density with Risk for Fracture

Merck and its competitors cranked out TV commercials and print ads about how their products could not only stop, but reverse osteoporosis. None of these featured any frail or humped elderly grandmothers, but rather attractive, youthful and athletic looking middle-aged women. Some ads even implied in a subtle fashion that they took these drugs to preserve this appearance as well as reverse osteoporosis. The Boniva blitz touted 60-year-old celebrity Sally Field, because her girlish fresh face looks gave the impression she was closer to 40. She also had a low bone density score that made her claims more legitimate.

As the Nobel Laureate Richard Feynman emphasized "I learned a long time ago the difference between knowing something and the name of something." This certainly applies to osteopenia, which is an artificial and completely invented condition that has no symptoms or signs. It is not a disease that requires treatment, there is no proof that it will progress to osteoporosis in the near future or that current drugs will help prevent this. The vast majority of people with osteoporosis also have no complaints other than age related loss of stature that usually does not impair quality of life. The goal of treatment is to prevent or decrease the likelihood of fractures, especially of the hip, and it is assumed that this can only be accomplished by increasing bone density. It is also assumed that if you have a bone density osteoporosis rating in the wrist or some other peripheral part of the body that there is likely a similar degree of osteoporosis in the hip and spine.

These and other speculations have been transformed into facts in deceptive ads despite the fact that they are not supported (and in many instances have been contradicted) by scientific studies. Boniva has been a bonanza because it targets the more than 40 million healthy middle-aged American women estimated to have osteopenia. Since Boniva is not indicated for this admittedly normal state, osteopenia is never mentioned in commercials. What Sally Field says is that "After 1 year on Boniva 9 out of 10 women have improved bone density." This is what osteopenic women want to hear, since most have been led to believe that they will soon develop osteoporosis, despite studies showing that they can remain in this category for ten or more years without medication. Boniva ads claiming to "reverse bone loss" in 90% of women after one year are based on the assumption that higher density means that their bones are stronger, which is also erroneous. . . .

The femur is the largest and strongest bone in the body, but these drugs reduce its strength and increase susceptibility to fractures.

More of these fractures have been seen with Fosamax because it has been around the longest, but similar breaks have been increasingly reported with Actonel, Boniva and Reclast. In some instances, simply walking up or down stairs can cause a break, and one 60-year-old woman fractured both her femurs. Many feel that all biphosphonates should carry a black box warning because physicians as well as patients are unaware of this growing problem or the dangers of taking these drugs for more than five years. The FDA warned Merck about reports of femur fractures in 2008, but it took 16 months for the company to respond, by simply adding six words to the list of possible side effects reported by patients, "low energy femoral shaft and subtrochanteric fractures." Neither the FDA nor Merck has made any other effort to inform physicians or the public about this growing menace.

All we see are deceptive ads claiming that Boniva can provide protection from hip fractures in women by up to 65%, and up to 50% for Fosamax. But these impressive statistics are from studies in elderly women with evidence of at least one vertebral fracture who are very likely to sustain a subsequent break. In the 3 year Fracture Intervention Trial, twice as many in the placebo group (2.2%) suffered a fracture, compared to 1.1% taking Fosamax, and since 1.1 is half of 2.2, Merck can claim a relative risk reduction of 50%. They don't tell you that the absolute risk reduction is 1.1 (2.2% minus 1.1%). Put another way, if 100 women took Fosamax for 3 years, it would prevent one from getting a fracture, but 99 would receive no benefit. As the old saying goes, "Figures don't lie—but liars can figure." The belief that increased bone density prevents hip fractures in the elderly is equally fallacious and misleading since over 90% are from falls due to loss of balance, coordination and rapid reflexes. Such falls could have had the same effect in younger people, but since osteoporosis is so common in senior citizens, there is a statistical association that has been exploited. In studies of elderly women at increased risk for hip fracture for reasons other than low bone density, biphosphonates provided absolutely no protection.

The reason most people, including doctors, believe that Boniva will prevent two thirds of hip fractures is a testimony to the power of pharmacracy advertising. As [English author] Lewis Carroll wrote, "What I tell you three times is true." He was referring to the snark, a mythical animal, but studies show that if you repeat anything several times and others spread this about, it is eventually accepted as being true. William James, the father of psychology noted, "There's nothing so absurd that if you repeat it often enough, people will believe it."

The Pharmaceutical Industry Influences Government, Consumers, and Medical Professionals

Drugwatch.com

Drugwatch.com is a resource about dangerous side effects and complications from commonly prescribed drugs and oft-used medical devices. Its mission is to educate people and help them evaluate whether they have a legal case because of those effects.

Big Pharma is the nickname given to the world's vast and influential pharmaceutical industry and its trade and lobbying group, the Pharmaceutical Research and Manufacturers of America or PhRMA.

The industry wields enormous influence over the prescription drug and medical device markets around the globe. In fact, in the United States the industry contributes heavily to the annual budget of the U.S. Food and Drug Administration (FDA), which is charged with regulating drugs and devices made by those same companies.

In addition, Big Pharma demonstrates its power, political might and social influence over the nation's governments and agencies, its health care systems, its doctors and hospitals, as well as the psyche of the American people. Because of the industry's 1,100-plus paid lobbyists on Capitol Hill, its $188 million annual lobbying budget and the $14 million or so it doles out to political candidates every year, the United States, which makes up 5 percent of the world's population, accounts for 34 percent of the money spent on prescription drugs.

In 2009, the world's 12 largest drug companies made a net profit of nearly $78 billion on revenues of $434 billion. (Seven of the 12 are headquartered in the United States: Johnson & Johnson, Pfizer, Abbot Laboratories, Merck, Wyeth, Bristol-Myers Squibb and Eli Lilly.) The next three dozen companies combined raked in $46 billion on revenues of $203 billion. By 2014, the global market for pharmaceuticals is expected to reach $1.1 trillion.

But the large amount of cash Big Pharma bestows on government representatives and on regulatory bodies is small when compared with the more than $4 billion it spends each year on direct-to-consumer advertising.

Prescription drugs and devices ... bring in billions in profits, but may leave consumers with serious adverse side effects.

For example, a single manufacturer, Boehringer Ingelheim, spent $464 million to advertise its blood thinner Pradaxa in 2011. The following year, Pradaxa passed the $1 billion sales mark. The money in this business appears to be well-spent.

The United States is one of only two countries in the world whose governments allow prescription drugs to be advertised on TV (the other is New Zealand).

When it comes to drugs taken and devices used by the American public, a handful of parent companies come into view: Pfizer, Johnson & Johnson, Merck, GlaxoSmithKline and Eli Lilly. A handful of other companies are also under a microscope because of recent drugs or devices whose effectiveness has come into question. Those companies include Bard, Stryker, Novartis and P&G.

Prescription drugs and devices manufactured by these companies bring in billions in profits, but may leave consumers with serious adverse side effects. The suffering experienced by users of the drugs and devices is hard to quantify....

How Does Big Pharma Work?

Critics contend that Big Pharma uses manipulative, ubiquitous and expensive advertising to sway lawmakers, the FDA and the public. Drug companies spend substantially more on marketing than they do on research and development, which in turn spurs on hypochondria [excessive concern about your health, including a tendency to imagine that you have illnesses that you do not actually have] and raises consumers' health fears.

The American public is not the only sector of society influenced by Big Pharma's techniques. Doctors, scientists and research organizations, medical journals, teaching hospitals and university medical schools all exhibit disturbing conflicts of interest between their publicly stated missions and their financial and ideological subservience to Big Pharma.

Doctors are still some of the most trusted people in our society. They study for many years, take an oath to "do no harm" and vow to depend only on accepted medical science to guide and support their professional conduct and decisions they make on behalf of patients.

But doctors complete some of their expert research with funds from Big Pharma. For instance, in 2007 the industry paid for more than half of the $100 billion that went into research.

Big Pharma Sways Opinions

Doctors may be persuaded to allow ghostwriting, which involves Big Pharma paying physicians to attach their names to a positive article about a particular drug with the goal of seeing it published in a reputable medical journal.

Often the commentary is little more than an advertisement penned by a company-paid copywriter showcasing a newer product. Ghostwriting was used to promote numerous drugs, including the antidepressant Paxil, the recalled weight loss drug Fen-Phen, the anti-epilepsy drug Neurontin, the antidepressant Zoloft, and painkiller Vioxx, to name a few.

Big Pharma tends to weaken the objectivity of even the most honest health professionals while encouraging them to over-prescribe medications.

In addition, even when a medical reviewer, who is an expert in the field, writes a comprehensive assessment of a new drug for a medical journal, it is common practice for those supposedly unbiased professionals to be on Big Pharma's payroll. In 1998, a study of the prestigious *New England Journal of Medicine* found that out of 75 published articles, nearly half were written by authors with financial conflicts. And, worse than this, only two of the articles disclosed interests.

Those medical journals are widely hailed as collections of unbiased scientific evaluation and separated from the long financial arm of pharmaceutical industry influence. Yet Richard Smith, former editor of the *British Medical Journal*, says, "All journals are bought—or at least cleverly used—by the pharmaceutical industry."

Big Pharma tends to weaken the objectivity of even the most honest health professionals while encouraging them to over-prescribe medications. Consider the numbers:

- *Advertising instead of research*: For every $1 spent on "basic research," Big Pharma spends $19 on promotions and advertising.

- *Distribution of free drug samples*: The United States has 1 pharmaceutical sales representative for every 5 office-based physicians.

- *Sponsorship of symposiums and medical conventions*: Drug and medical device makers spend lavishly on doctors, including covering meals, travel, seminars and conventions that may look more like vacations.

It is not uncommon for Big Pharma to pull its ads when those same journals question the accuracy of an advertisement, or run an article contrary to Big Pharma's agenda. That kind of hardball intimidation has a chilling effect on editors and publishers who must weigh their scientific objectivity with the requirements of running a business, especially when Big Pharma can make up the vast bulk of a journal's advertising revenue.

Indeed, many medical journals, including the esteemed *Journal of the American Medical Association*, actively vie for the attention of Big Pharma advertising dollars, billing themselves as the best way for drug companies to reach their professional readership.

Big Pharma and Researchers

Then there are medical researchers, who are hardly immune to Big Pharma's financial power. Because drug companies are the principal sponsors of the clinical trials that researchers are paid to administer, too often the academics and scientists are hired hands who supply human subjects and collect data according to the instructions from their corporate employers. Sponsors keep the data, analyze it, write the papers and decide whether and when and where to submit them for publication.

Drug companies have discovered ways to stage-manage trials to produce predetermined outcomes that will put their products in the best light.

Bad drugs can be made to look good by:

- Comparing them to a placebo

- Comparing them to a competitor's medication in the wrong strength

- Pairing them with a drug that is known to work well

- Shortening a trial before any bad results surface

- Testing in groups too small to provide valid evidence

Another popular research trick is the technique of "data mining," wherein small subgroups of an unsuccessful trial are scrutinized in search of any group for whom a benefit does emerge, or seems to.

Doctors not only receive biased information but learn a drug-intensive style of medicine. They come to believe that there is a drug for everything.

Finally there is selective presentation. A company may conduct 1,000 trials. If two are positive, they get FDA approval and are published. The other 998 never see the light of day.

Medical Schools and Big Pharma

Big Pharma also infiltrated medical schools. Teachers, department chairs and deans are known to sit on drug companies' boards of directors, and that influences educational content. Money from Big Pharma supports programs within many medical schools and teaching hospitals, and company reps are given access to young doctors to promote their wares.

The result is doctors not only receive biased information but learn a drug-intensive style of medicine. They come to believe that there is a drug for everything and that new drugs (of which they have many free samples) are always better than old ones.

In most states, doctors must also take accredited education courses, called continuing medical education (CME). The pharmaceutical industry provides a substantial proportion of the billions spent on CME annually and continues to use that support as a marketing tool.

In addition, academic centers are able to receive royalties from Big Pharma on any drug or technology they help to create and patent as a result of research, sometimes underwritten with government funds. Columbia University, for example, received nearly $300 million from more than 30 biotech companies during the 17-year life of its medical school's patent on a method for synthesizing certain biological products.

There are hopes that the future of Big Pharma will change, since President [Barack] Obama's Affordable Care Act requires that starting in September 2013, companies will need to collect data and openly report information on payments, investment interests, ownership and items of value given to doctors and hospitals—but this is only a small step.

Lawsuits also reveal monetary persuasion offered to doctors. For example, two patients receiving faulty hips made by Stryker discovered that the surgeon who implanted the devices had been given $225,000 to $250,000 from the manufacturer for "consultation services."

Big Pharma appears less interested in the health of the American public than it is in fulfilling its fiduciary responsibility to its shareholders. And because Big Pharma's influence is so extensive, and self-interest is the motive of its giant network, the well-being of society may be in serious jeopardy.

So Young and So Many Pills

Anna Wilde Mathews

Anna Wilde Mathews is a health reporter for the Wall Street Journal.

Gage Martindale, who is 8 years old, has been taking a blood-pressure drug since he was a toddler. "I want to be healthy, and I don't want things in my heart to go wrong," he says.

And, of course, his mom is always there to check Gage's blood pressure regularly with a home monitor, and to make sure the second-grader doesn't skip a dose of his once-a-day enalapril.

These days, the medicine cabinet is truly a family affair. More than a quarter of U.S. kids and teens are taking a medication on a chronic basis, according to Medco Health Solutions Inc., the biggest U.S. pharmacy-benefit manager with around 65 million members. Nearly 7% are on two or more such drugs, based on the company's database figures for 2009.

Doctors and parents warn that prescribing medications to children can be problematic. There is limited research available about many drugs' effects in kids. And health-care providers and families need to be vigilant to assess the medicines' impact, both intended and not. Although the effects of some medications, like cholesterol-lowering statins, have been extensively researched in adults, the consequences of using such drugs for the bulk of a patient's lifespan are little understood.

Many medications kids take on a regular basis are well known, including treatments for asthma and attention-deficit hyperactivity disorder [ADHD].

But children and teens are also taking a wide variety of other medications once considered only to be for adults, from statins to diabetes pills and sleep drugs, according to figures provided to the *Wall Street Journal* by IMS Health, a research firm. Prescriptions for antihypertensives in people age 19 and younger could hit 5.5 million this year [2010] if the trend though September continues, according to IMS. That would be up 17% from 2007, the earliest year available.

Children's reactions to medicines can be very different than those of adults. Long-term effects of drugs in kids are almost never known.

Researchers attribute the wide usage in part to doctors and parents becoming more aware of drugs as an option for kids. Unhealthy diets and lack of exercise among children, which lead to too much weight gain and obesity, also fuel the use of some treatments, such as those for hypertension. And some conditions are likely caught and treated earlier as screening and diagnosis efforts improve.

Gage, who isn't overweight, has been on hypertension drugs since he had surgery to fix a heart defect as a toddler, says his mother, Stefanie Martindale, a Conway, Ark., marketing-company manager.

Most medications that could be prescribed to children on a chronic basis haven't been tested specifically in kids, says Danny Benjamin, a Duke University pediatrics professor. And older drugs rarely get examined, since pharmaceutical firms have little incentive to test medicines once they are no longer under patent protection.

Still, a growing number of studies have been done under a Food and Drug Administration [FDA] program that rewards drug companies for testing medications in children. In more than a third of these studies, there have been surprising side effects, or results that suggested a smaller or larger dose was needed than had been expected, Dr. Benjamin says. Those findings underscore that children's reactions to medicines can be very different than those of adults. Long-term effects of drugs in kids are almost never known, since pediatric studies, like those in adults, tend to be relatively short.

"We know we're making errors in dosing and safety," says Dr. Benjamin, who is leading a new National Institutes of Health [NIH] initiative to study drugs in children. He suggests that parents should do as much research as they can to understand the evidence for the medicine, confirm the diagnosis, and identify side effects. Among the places to check: drug labels and other resources on the FDA's website, published research at www.pubmed.gov, and clinical guidelines from groups like the American Academy of Pediatrics.

When a child psychiatrist diagnosed their then 8-year-old daughter with bipolar disorder four years ago, Ken and Joy Lewis, of Chapel Hill, N.C., sought a second opinion from another child psychiatrist.

They also worked with a psychologist. Dr. [Ken] Lewis, who leads a company that does early-stage drug studies, reads all the available research on each medication suggested for the girl, now 12, who has taken antipsychotics and other psychiatric medications including Risperdal and Haldol.

"If your child has a chronic problem, then you have to invest the time as a parent," he says.

Parents and doctors also say nondrug alternatives should be explored where possible. Tom Wells, a professor of pediatrics at the University of Arkansas for Medical Sciences who sees patients at Arkansas Children's Hospital in Little Rock, frequently pushes diet and exercise changes before drugs for hypertensive kids. "Obesity is really the biggest cause I see for high blood pressure in adolescents," he says. But only about 10% of families adhere to his diet and exercise recommendations, he says.

Beverly Pizzano, a psychologist who lives in Palm Harbor, Fla., spent years struggling with behavioral therapies for her son Steven, 10, who showed symptoms of ADHD at a young age. She worked with a counselor on a system of rewards for good behavior, and even had a research team watch him and suggest interventions. But she turned to medications after he struggled in kindergarten. "We tried everything before I would get to that," she says.

After a drug is prescribed, children must be closely monitored, doctors say. They may not recognize or communicate a possible side effect, or whether their symptoms are improving. They also don't always follow prescription instructions.

Robert Lemanske, a professor at the University of Wisconsin in Madison, says patients at his pediatric asthma clinic are checked regularly for side effects such as slowed rates of growth. He quizzes parents and young patients on details like where they keep their inhalers to make sure they're taking their prescribed medicine.

Nichole Ramsey, a preschool teacher whose 9-year-old son Antwone is a patient at the clinic, watches her son's basketball practices so she can head off any wheezing or other symptoms. She also makes sure she's around when he gets his regular Advair dose. If Antwone stays at a friend's house overnight, she asks the parents to watch that he takes steps like rinsing out his mouth to avoid a fungal infection that can be a side effect of the inhaled drug.

"You're still the best monitor of what's going on with them," she says of a parent's role.

Ms. Ramsey is particularly concerned about Advair, which has been tied to rare instances of asthma-related death, but says it works better than a previous drug he was using. Before he started the medications, Antwone was hospitalized several times for asthma attacks.

As children's bodies change and grow, they often need different drugs or doses, says Greg Kearns, chairman of medical research at Children's Mercy Hospital in Kansas City, Mo.

Jennifer Flory, a homemaker in Baldwin City, Kan., says that after her daughter Cassandra, now 16, started taking a higher dose of the asthma drug Singulair a few years ago, she became more moody and sad. Ms. Flory didn't connect the change to the drug, but when she eventually mentioned it to a nurse practitioner at the girl's asthma clinic, the nurse suggested stopping Singulair, which currently has a precaution in its label about possible psychiatric side effects. Cassandra, who continued taking Advair, became far more cheerful and didn't have any increase in asthma symptoms, Ms. Flory says.

A spokesman for Merck & Co., which makes Singulair, said in a statement that the company is "confident in the efficacy and safety of Singulair," which is "an important treatment option for appropriate patients."

Insufficient or Improper Use of Prescription Drugs Wastes Billions of Dollars

Christian Nordqvist

Christian Nordqvist is the chief executive officer and editor-in-chief of Medical News Today.

The American healthcare system overspends by $200 billion, 8% of its healthcare budget, because medications are not being used responsibly by doctors and patients every year, says a new report issued by the IMS Institute for Healthcare Informatics.

Irresponsible medication usage causes millions of avoidable outpatient treatments, emergency room visits, drug prescriptions and hospital admissions.

According to the *Wall Street Journal*, the cost of building the One World Trade Center, the skyscraper under construction at Ground Zero in New York, is approximately $4 billion. Therefore, medication misuse in the United States costs the equivalent of 50 One World Trade Center skyscrapers every year, or 500 of them in one decade.

The authors of the report focused on six areas that push up healthcare costs unnecessarily:

- *Medication non-adherence* (non-compliance)—the patient forgets to take the medication, or does not complete the course.

- *Delayed evidence-based treatment practice*—treatments that are scientifically proven to be effective are not administered promptly.

- *Medication errors*—the wrong medicine is prescribed, the drug is administered incorrectly, failure to prescribe the correct medication, usage of outdated drugs, lack of awareness of the adverse effects of some medication combinations.

- *Underusing generic drugs*—not using cheaper generic drugs. Generic drugs are just as effective as brand names, the active ingredient is the same, but generics are much cheaper.

- *Misuse of antibiotics*—prescribing antibiotics when there is no infection, or viral infections (antibiotics are for bacterial infections only). Also known as antibiotic abuse or antibiotic overuse.

  Antibiotic resistance is a growing problem, not just for healthcare costs, but also public health. Antibiotic resistance has become a major threat to public health around the world, and for the large part, the cause is misuse of antibiotics, the European Centre for Disease Prevention and Control concluded in a report.

- *Mismanagement of multiple medications* (polypharmacy) in older patients—often inappropriate for older adults, because the risks outweigh the benefits.

These six areas use up enormous healthcare resources unnecessarily, involving an estimated four million emergency room visits, 246 million prescriptions, 78 million outpatients treatments, and 10 million hospitalizations every year.

Reducing Wasteful Costs

The authors said that there are numerous ways of reducing these wasteful costs while at the same time making sure that patients receive the right medications . . . and take them according to instructions.

Murray Aitken, executive director, IMS Institute for Healthcare Informatics, said "As our study makes clear, drugs are often not used optimally, resulting in significant unnecessary health system spending and patient burdens. Those avoidable costs could pay for the healthcare of more than 24 million currently uninsured U.S. citizens. Reaching a meaningful level of consensus and alignment among stakeholders, based on measured and proven success models, is a key step to unlocking the $200 billion opportunity identified in our study."

When a patient does not follow the doctor's medication guidance, the risk of complications rises, complications push up healthcare costs.

The report—*Avoidable Costs in U.S. Healthcare: The $200 Billion Opportunity from Using Medicines More Responsibly*— identified some areas where wasteful spending is being addressed.

Drug adherence among patients with diabetes, hypertension and hyperlipidemia has improved 3% to 4% since 2009. In 2007, twenty percent of patients with flu were prescribed antibiotics compared to just 6% today. In 2013, ninety-five percent of patients receive cheaper generic alternatives to brand medications (when available).

The report's findings are highlighted below:

- *Medication nonadherence*—cause $105 billion in avoidable healthcare costs every year. When a patient does not follow the doctor's medication guidance, the risk of complications rises, complications push up healthcare costs.

  There are several underlying reasons for nonadherence. However, the increasing usage of analytics, plus better collaboration among pharmacists, providers and patients seems to be improving, which in turn helps patients understand the effectiveness of intervention programs.

- *Delayed evidence-based treatment practices*—leads to about $40 billion in extra costs. The authors identified four disease areas, including diabetes, where patients were diagnosed too late, or treatment did not start straight away after diagnosis. Delay in diabetes diagnosis and treatment drives up costs the most.

    If insurance coverage were expanded, and more patients at high risk of developing diabetes were screened regularly, avoidable costs would be reduced considerably.

- *Misuse of antibiotics*—is estimated to be responsible for about $34 billion in avoidable inpatient care costs. Furthermore, another $1 billion is wasted on approximately 31 million inappropriate antibiotic prescriptions that are dispensed annually, in most cases for viral infections.

    However, efforts to promote responsible antibiotic usage appear to be working. The number of prescriptions given for flu and the common cold has dropped. Flu and colds are viral infections, viral infections do not respond to antibiotics.

The authors wrote:

"Many efforts are underway to address the underlying causes of avoidable spending and to improve medication use. A large number of initiatives are advancing across the healthcare landscape, including novel interventions, critical assessments of established solutions and pioneering models of stakeholder cooperation.

Many of these initiatives involve a greater role for pharmacists, an integrated approach to addressing patient issues, alignment of financial incentives, and greater use of health-care informatics to guide decision-making and monitor progress."

Giving Drugs to Healthy People Can Prevent Them from Developing Serious Illness

Dean Herbert

Dean Herbert is a reporter for the Scottish Daily Express.

Pills that lower cholesterol should be prescribed to healthy patients to prevent them from developing life-threatening heart disease, experts said yesterday [July 2013].

Groundbreaking new research carried out by Scottish experts found that prescribing statins to healthy patients can significantly reduce their chances of suffering a heart attack or stroke.

Researchers say that by using statins as a preventative measure against heart disease, the NHS [British National Health Service] would save millions of pounds a year in treatment costs.

The pills are usually only prescribed to patients who already have high cholesterol, have developed cardiovascular disease or have suffered heart attacks or strokes. Separate studies have found that statins reduce the chances of dying early by up to 70 per cent, leading to calls for everyone over 50 to be prescribed the drugs.

Now researchers at the University of Glasgow say they have proved that widespread use of statins by otherwise healthy people carries clear financial and health benefits.

A major study which followed 6,595 middle-aged men from the west of Scotland for 15 years found that those who took the cholesterol-lowering pravastatin drug were far less likely to need hospital treatment for heart disease and stroke.

For every 1,000 patients who received a 40mg dose once a day for five years, the NHS saved £710,000, after taking into account the cost of the drug and safety monitoring.

There were also 163 fewer admissions, saving 1,836 days in hospital, with fewer admissions for heart attacks, stroke and coronary operations.

There was also a 43 per cent reduction in heart failure admissions to hospital over the 15-year period amongst those who were given the drug.

Estimated Cost Savings

With nearly 250,000 Scots currently living with heart disease, and more than 100,000 with stroke, prescribing statins could save the NHS millions of pounds in the future.

Dr Andrew Walker, health economist at the Robertson Centre for Biostatics at the university, said last night: "The results from this study are clear—treatment with a statin in middle age saves lives and frees up NHS beds for other patients."

A 10-year study of 10,000 people in the US revealed a combination of statins and regular exercise decrease the likelihood of dying younger from heart disease by 70 per cent.

It is the first time the cost-effectiveness of prescribing statins on a large scale has been scientifically assessed. It is estimated that statins cost around 40p [pence] per day for each patient.

The men who took part in the study all had high levels of cholesterol, but no history of a heart attack.

Professor Naveed Sattar, Professor of Metabolic Medicine at the Institute of Cardiovascular and Medical Sciences, said:

"These carefully determined results suggest that generic statins are highly cost-effective in [a] primary prevention setting."

Last year, a 10-year study of 10,000 people in the US revealed a combination of statins and regular exercise decrease[d] the likelihood of dying younger from heart disease by 70 per cent. Italian researchers also published research showing that statins dramatically cut the chance of developing deadly liver cancer.

Concerns had previously been raised that statins increase the chances of kidney damage after a heart attack. But studies have found that this occurs in very few people who use the drugs.

More than eight million people in the UK [United Kingdom] take statins daily and experts say that if five million more took them it would cut heart attacks and stroke by 10,000 a year, saving 2,000 lives.

The most commonly prescribed brand, simvastatin, and another, pravastatin, appear to be the safest, with the fewest side effects. This is particularly true when patients were prescribed low to moderate doses.

Pharmacists Key to Improving Mediocre Medication Adherence Levels

Daniel Weiss

Daniel Weiss is a senior editor of Pharmacy Times.

A mericans who take prescription drugs for chronic conditions are falling short when it comes to medication adherence, according to a report released on June 25, 2013, by the National Community Pharmacists Association (NCPA). The report, titled "Medication Adherence in America: A National Report Card," also finds that having a strong sense of personal connection with pharmacists is an important predictor of whether patients are adherent.

The report was based on a survey carried out by Langer Research Associates. It was conducted between February 20 and March 10, 2013, and included 1020 adults aged 40 and older who had been prescribed medications for a chronic condition. Participants were asked whether they had engaged in any of 9 non-adherent behaviors over the previous 12 months: failing to fill or refill a prescription, missing a dose, taking a lower or higher dose than prescribed, stopping taking a prescription early, taking an old medication for a new problem without consulting a doctor, taking someone else's medication, or forgetting whether they had taken a medication. Participants were also asked questions about their relationships with health care providers and their attitudes toward their health and their prescription medications.

Participants' adherence level was calculated on a scale of 0 (non-adherence on all 9 behaviors) to 100 (adherence on all 9 behaviors). Overall, 24% of respondents received an A grade for reporting complete adherence; another 24% received a B grade for being largely adherent, reporting on average 1 non-adherent behavior; 20% received a C grade for reporting an average of 2 non-adherent behaviors; 16% received a D grade for reporting an average of 3 non-adherent behaviors; and the remaining 15% were largely non-adherent and received an F grade, with an average of 4 or more non-adherent behaviors.

"Proper prescription drug use can improve patient health outcomes and lower health care costs, so anything less than an A on medication adherence is concerning," said NCPA CEO [chief executive officer] B. Douglas Hoey, RPh, MBA, in a press release. "Pharmacists can help patients and caregivers overcome barriers to effectively and consistently follow medication regimens. Indeed, independent community pharmacists in particular may be well-suited to boost patient adherence given their close connection with patients and their caregivers."

The most common forms of non-adherence reported by participants were missing a dose (57%), forgetting whether they had taken their medication (30%), failing to refill a prescription on time (28%), taking a lower dose than instructed (22%), and failing to refill a new prescription (20%). The most common reasons cited for non-adherence were forgetting to take medication (42%), running out of medication (34%), being away from home (27%), attempting to save money (22%), unpleasant side effects (21%), being too busy (17%), feeling that medication was not working (17%), believing that medication was not needed (16%), and disliking taking medication (12%).

Analysis of the participants' responses found 6 key predictors of adherence: having a personal connection with one's pharmacist or pharmacy staff; affordability of medications; level of continuity in health care; patients' sense of the importance of taking medication exactly as prescribed; how well informed patients felt about their health; and the level of medications' unpleasant side effects. These predictors suggest that adherence can be improved by creating a stronger personal connection between patients and pharmacy staff, increasing patients' level of health information and awareness of the importance of adherence, and encouraging patients to discuss side effects when they occur.

There is room for improvement in the frequency with which pharmacists discuss new prescriptions with patients.

Personal Connection with Pharmacy Staff

The 63% of respondents who reported that their pharmacist or pharmacy staff knew them "pretty well" had an average adherence grade of 80, compared with 77 for those without this sense of connectedness. The report authors note that this is a slight difference, but is statistically significant and that after controlling for other factors, a sense of connectedness with one's pharmacist or pharmacy staff was the survey's "single strongest individual predictor of medication adherence."

The type of pharmacy that a patient used played a major role in determining whether they felt a strong sense of connectedness to its staff. Of mail-order pharmacy users, 36% reported that their pharmacist or pharmacy staff knew them pretty well, compared with 67% of chain pharmacy users and 89% of neighborhood pharmacy users.

The portion of patients who felt that the pharmacist or pharmacy staff knew them pretty well also increased with the duration of a prescription: 38% for those who received their first prescription within the last 2 years, 60% for those who had been prescribed a medication for 3 to 5 years, and 68% for those had been prescribed a medication for 6 years or longer. Patients' sense of connectedness to pharmacy staff was slightly higher in the Midwest and Northeast than in other parts of the country and was higher in suburban and rural areas than in urban areas.

Patients were more likely to see adherence as important when they felt that their medication was helping them to live a better or longer life.

The results also indicate that pharmacists are less likely than doctors to speak with patients about new prescriptions: 77% of respondents said that their physicians always do so, compared with nearly 6 in 10 who say their pharmacist always does this—48% for mail-order pharmacy users and 61% for chain or independent pharmacy users. This suggests that there is room for improvement in the frequency with which pharmacists discuss new prescriptions with patients.

"Pharmacists have a role at the forefront of addressing prescription medication non-adherence," write the report authors. "The results of this survey indicate that much depends on the extent to which pharmacists and pharmacy staff establish a personal connection with their customers and engage with them to encourage fuller understanding of the importance of taking medications as prescribed. Independent pharmacists may be particularly well-placed to boost adherence, given their greater personal connection with patients."

Sense of Adherence Importance

For the half of respondents who considered it extremely important to take their medication exactly as prescribed, the average adherence score was 81, compared with 77 for those who saw this as less important. Patients were more likely to see adherence as important when they felt that their medication was helping them to live a better or longer life, when adherence was perceived as easy to achieve, when they had no concern about the long-term effects of medication, and when they felt a strong sense of personal connection with pharmacy staff. In addition, 55% of patients with hypertension said that following prescription instructions was extremely important, compared with 42% of those with other conditions.

Medication Affordability

Respondents who said it was very easy to afford their medications had an average adherence score of 83, compared with 74 for those who reported difficulty covering their medication costs.

Medication Side Effects

For the 3 in 10 respondents who reported having at least some unpleasant medication side effects, the average adherence score was 74, compared with 83 for the half of respondents who reported no unpleasant side effects.

Continuity of Care

Nearly 70% of respondents reported seeing the same health care provider for each doctor's visit, and they had an average adherence score of 81, compared with an average of 75 for those who saw the same provider most of the time or less frequently.

Health Information level

For the 8 in 10 respondents who reported feeling very informed about their health, the average adherence score was 80, compared with 74 for those who felt less informed.

Age

Older respondents were generally more adherent; those aged 50 and older had an average adherence score of 81, compared with 73 for those under 50.

CHAPTER 2

Are Prescription Drug Prices Unjustifiably High?

Overview: Many Factors Influence the Cost of Prescription Drugs

Henry J. Kaiser Family Foundation

The Henry J. Kaiser Family Foundation is a nonprofit organization focused on health policy analysis, health journalism, and communication.

Advances in pharmaceutical treatments have transformed health care over the last several decades. Today, many health problems are prevented, cured, or managed effectively for years through the use of prescription drugs. In some cases, the use of prescription medicines keeps people from needing other expensive health care interventions, such as hospitalization or surgery. In 2010, 90% of seniors and 57% of non-elderly adults had a prescription drug expense. Additionally, the number of medicines being prescribed has increased: from 1999 to 2011, the number of prescriptions rose 43% (from 2.8 billion to 4 billion), outpacing U.S. population growth of 9%. Although still only a modest part of total health care spending in the U.S (10%), with so many people relying on prescriptions, the cost implications loom large for the American public, health insurers, and government payers.

Manufacturing and development of new drugs and patent protection laws are two of the major factors that influence drug spending. Drug manufacturers increase drug costs to try to recoup the often significant outlays in research and development costs for drugs that make it to the market as well as those that do not enter the marketplace. Additionally, drug manufacturers make substantial investments in marketing practices, to influence physician prescribing habits and consumer demand for newer more expensive drugs. Furthermore, patent protection laws provide manufacturers an exclusive right to sell a new drug product for up to 20 years, after which the drug may be manufactured in generic versions by other manufacturers, lowering the selling price.

More than one in ten (11.2%) of adults between 18 and 64 reported that they went without or delayed filling a prescription medication because of the costs.

Spending in the U.S. for prescription drugs was $259.1 billion in 2010, and is projected to double over the next decade. The current rate of growth has slowed from the highs of the 1990s and early 2000s to a more modest rate, but is expected to increase sharply in 2014 after the implementation of the Affordable Care Act (ACA). The recent slowdown in spending growth is attributable to a number of factors including slower growth in the utilization of drugs, increased use of generic drugs which cost less, the loss of patent protection for brand-name drugs such as Lipitor and Plavix, an increase in Medicaid prescription drug rebates, and a decrease in the number of new drugs introduced.

Public and Private Spending on Drugs

Historically, private plans and public insurers have responded to rising prescription drug costs by increasing enrollee cost-sharing amounts, using formularies to exclude certain drugs from coverage, applying quantity dispensing limits, requiring prior authorization, and using step therapy (starting with the most cost-effective drug and progressing to more costly therapy only if necessary). Private plans and Medicaid programs negotiate with pharmaceutical manufacturers to receive discounts and rebates that are applied based on volume, prompt payment, and market share.

Nearly all private health insurance plans cover prescription medicines; however, there is considerable variation in the drugs that are covered and the share of costs that the insured individual must bear. The vast majority of covered workers (87%) are in plans where policyholders pay different cost-sharing amounts for different classifications of drugs (generic, preferred, non-preferred) called "tiering." While this can encourage consumers and their providers to use less expensive drugs, it can be problematic to low-income individuals, who may not be able to afford the higher co-payments charged for preferred medications which usually include brand-name drugs without a generic substitute. More than one in ten (11.2%) of adults between 18 and 64 reported that they went without or delayed filling a prescription medication because of the costs.

The Medicare Part D outpatient prescription drug benefit went into effect on January 1, 2006. Before this program, Medicare did not cover prescription drugs and beneficiaries either obtained coverage through supplemental plans or through Medicaid if they were dually eligible for both programs. Spending on the Part D program is estimated to have reached $60 billion in 2011 by Congressional budget analysis. While subsidies are available for low-income seniors for the associated costs of Part D, some Medicare beneficiaries still incur significant out-of-pocket expenses for their prescription drugs due to a gap in coverage which is often referred to as the Part D "donut hole." The ACA will also help reduce out-of-pocket costs for Medicare beneficiaries by gradually closing the "donut hole."

Medicaid is the major source of outpatient prescription drugs for the low-income population and people with HIV/AIDS. While all state Medicaid programs cover prescription drugs, there are important differences in state policies with regard to copayments charged to enrollees, preferred drugs, and the number of prescriptions that can be filled. Prescription drug coverage accounted for 6.6% of total Medicaid spending in 2009 and 10% of total prescription drug spending in the U.S. There are also federal policies that help lower prescription drug costs under Medicaid, including the Section 340B Program, which requires manufacturers to provide drugs to certain providers such as community health centers at discounted prices as well as pharmaceutical company rebates to states for a portion of their Medicaid outpatient drug costs.

Looking Ahead

Access to coverage and the resulting use of prescription drugs will be expanded by the ACA's health insurance mandate. Prescription drug coverage is one of the "essential health benefits" that must be included in health plans in state-based health insurance exchanges and in the benchmark benefit packages for newly eligible adults under Medicaid. The law increases Medicaid drug rebate percentages for several types of outpatient drugs and requires that the resulting savings be remitted to the federal government. The ACA is expected to improve coverage and reduce cost-sharing for seniors through the closing of the "donut hole" and other regulatory changes. The health reform law also makes a number of other changes that will affect drug costs, such as requirements for pharmaceutical companies to include additional information in labeling and advertising to help consumers make more informed health care choices.

In years 2015 through 2021, drug spending growth is expected to average 6.6% per year, reflecting the diminishing impact on spending from more patent expirations and the greater use of generic drugs. This is only slightly higher than projected average growth rates of hospital care (6.2%) and physician and clinical services (6.2%). Spending on prescription drugs will continue to be influenced by increasing use of generic drugs and patent expiration for "blockbuster" drugs, as well as growth in drug utilization and new therapeutic biologics and molecular entities entering the market.

Pharmaceutical Companies Make Too Much Profit on Expensive Drugs

Mary Hiers

Mary Hiers is a writer with a background in engineering and print journalism who focuses on health-care topics.

High prices for prescription drugs affect most Americans. Those who do not have prescription drug coverage as part of their health insurance (and those who do not have health insurance) can end up spending significant chunks of their income for necessary prescription medications.

Those with prescription drug coverage feel the effects less, but they also face drug co-payments that have increased significantly, particularly for newer drugs for which generic alternatives don't exist.

Drug development is increasingly expensive. Despite technological advances, the number of new drugs per billion dollars spent on research and development has been cut in half every decade since 1950. But in some cases, consumers and even physicians have protested what they see as pharmaceutical companies crossing the line from profiting into profiteering.

Doctors specializing in a type of cancer called chronic myeloid leukemia (CML) published a commentary in *Blood, the Journal of the American Society of Hematology* stating that the prices of drugs used to treat CML are so high as to border on immoral. An extremely effective drug made by Novartis called Gleevec entered the market in 2001 and cost about $30,000 per year in the US then. Since that time, the price has tripled, despite competition from newer drugs, which cost even more than Gleevec.

Pharmaceutical research focuses on lucrative rather than most-needed products. This is disastrous for the global poor.

Despite drug company programs for those who can't afford the drugs, the commentary notes that in developing nations, cancer specialists actually proposed bone marrow transplants—a risky, grueling one-time treatment—because it costs less than continuous treatment with drugs like Gleevec. The American patent on Gleevec expires in 2015, which should provide some price relief. Novartis, however, is encouraging physicians to switch patients to Tasigna, a newer drug still under patent.

Neglected Diseases in Developing Nations

Last March [2013], [billionaire philanthropist and founder of Microsoft] Bill Gates spoke to the Royal Academy of Engineers in London [United Kingdom] concerning diseases in developing nations, saying, "Our priorities are tilted by marketplace imperatives. The malaria vaccine, in humanist terms, is the biggest need, but it gets virtually no funding. If you are working on male baldness or the other things you get an order of magnitude more research funding because of the voice in the marketplace."

In other words, pharmaceutical research focuses on lucrative rather than most-needed products. This is disastrous for the global poor, because their diseases aren't profitable enough to attract R&D [research and development] interest. These "Neglected Diseases," like Chagas disease, malaria, Dengue fever, river blindness, and tuberculosis, don't prompt research despite massive suffering in developing nations. Where drugs exist, they are often too expensive to be practical, or require sustained treatment over long periods to be effective.

Basic pharmaceutical R&D has traditionally taken place within silos, where there is little communication across labs, let alone across companies. This lack of information sharing means labs may be hamstrung by problems other researchers have already solved. Private and governmental agencies around the world are proposing new R&D paradigms that could avoid some of these problems. One suggestion is the use of cash prizes—rather than patents—for cures for neglected diseases. Once the cure is proven and the prize awarded, the cure would exist as open-access intellectual property, allowing manufacturers worldwide to compete to manufacture the drug cost effectively.

Some members of the World Health Organization have proposed an open platform for researchers in different locations in the world to pool data and coordinate work. Funding grants would require that the research exist on a public "observatory" that's cloud-hosted and openly accessible. Private researchers have already tried similar approaches. For example, an open source malaria project in Australia attracted the attention of a post-doctoral student in Scotland, who tracked the project's open lab books online. The post-doc student was able to synthesize a compound that the researchers in Australia were having difficulty with. The two laboratories interacted mostly through Twitter.

Will Public (and Physician) Outcry Help?

In at least one case, physician outcry over the cost of cancer drugs has made a difference. In the fall of 2012, physicians at New York's Memorial Sloan-Kettering Cancer Center refused to use a new drug for colon cancer called Zaltrap. Zaltrap had not been shown to be more effective than an existing drug for colon cancer, yet it cost twice as much. The Sloan-Kettering physicians went public in a *New York Times* op-ed article, and the manufacturer of Zaltrap, Sanofi, later dropped the price by half.

Zaltrap, however, was an unusual case, because an alternative, equally-effective drug already existed, and the cost of Zaltrap was particularly steep at over $11,000 per month. While physicians may feel more empowered by the actions of the doctors at Sloan-Kettering and those who wrote the commentary on CML drugs, physician outcry is not likely to be a big factor in reducing drug prices for the typical American. However, these actions could plant the seeds for dialogue among physicians, patients, and pharmaceutical companies about just how profitable drugs need to be to sustain continuing research and development.

Prescription Drugs Cost What the Market Will Bear

Jessica Wapner

Jessica Wapner is a writer focused mainly on biomedical issues whose work has appeared in many major national publications.

Few are the people who have not wondered why drugs cost what they do and, when the price tag has a pinch, sighed with exasperation. We've all read countless reports on the time- and resource-consuming labor of research and development. Elaborate studies have been done to count up (and debunk) all the dollars spent on creating new drugs. Even reports enumerating all the various pharma expenses still explain the price of prescription drugs by looking at what companies spend. And we've all read (or had our own) complaints: if only drug companies would advertise less, the price would go down. If only drug companies stopped wining and dining physicians, the price would go down. If only CEOs [chief executive officers] weren't so greedy. But here's the thing: none of this explains the price of medications.

So what is the great, big secret about why drugs cost what they do? Read on.

Drugs cost what the market will bear. It's that simple. Drug prices are set at whatever the market will bear.

So what does that mean? It means that if no one purchased a drug that cost $X, then the price would be lowered. Prices are set at exactly—and I mean *exactly*—at what the consumer/insurance infrastructure is able to carry.

It would be wrong to say that the prices reflect what we are willing to pay because for the most part, we don't pay the price tag; we pay for our insurance and then the co-pay amount for a given prescription. Of course this insight is referring to prescription drugs. When it comes to, say, headache medicine on the drugstore shelves, then the price more closely reflects what the customer is "willing to pay," the economic counterpart to "what the market will bear." But once we get into the domain of prescriptions, prices are guided by the market.

Complicated Calculations

As simple as that explanation is, the calculations behind the price are complicated. They factor in how many people will buy a drug, how many of those people are likely to be privately insured, how many are likely to have Medicare or Medicaid, how many will have no insurance at all, for how long will a given patient be on the drug (on average), how much it costs to make the drug (yes, this does matter), and even what's at stake (is the drug treating a life-or-death condition, or is it treating something more mild?).

Only when enough people can't afford their co-pays to upset the profit margin will the price [of prescription drugs] be lowered.

Also important is the number of years that a drug will have market exclusivity and whether exclusivity can be extended through any of a number of legal loopholes. Even patient assistance factors in. Everyone has heard the gently spoken words at the end of a prescription drug commercial: "If you can't afford your medication, drug company X may be able to help." These "patient assistance programs" are vital for assuring that people without insurance do not go without needed medications. But they are also part of the pricing strategy (a topic for a very juicy future post). There are companies that specialize in such forecasting, helping drug makers to decide on a price.

As convoluted as those calculations may be, the fact itself is simple: drugs cost what they do because that's what they can. (As one insider once told me, cancer drug prices could be lower, but they don't need to be.) This explains why different procedures cost different amounts in different places. It also explains why drug prices are different for taxpayer-funded insurance than for private insurance than for the uninsured.

The minute enough people stop filling prescriptions because they are too expensive, the prices will be lowered. The science is exact. Yes, there are plenty of people who do not fill their prescriptions because even with insurance, the price is still unaffordable. That's not good, but in the clear-cut economics of market-driven health care, only when enough people can't afford their co-pays to upset the profit margin will the price be lowered. And remember, private insurers are businesses, and are also part of the market equation.

Drug companies justify prices with the high cost of R&D [research and development] because stating outright that the prices are simply what the market will bear would look very bad. But consumers complaining about advertisements, etc. is equally unproductive. Drug companies advertise because the amount of profits guaranteed by what the market will bear allows them to advertise, which of course in turn increases earnings. Consumers are still at the whim of the corporate wheels, but also need to acknowledge the fact of the role that consumers play in the market.

So there you have it, the big secret behind the price of prescription drugs: they cost what the market will bear. Interesting, isn't it?

Prescription Drug Prices Are Increased by Unnecessary Regulations

Devon M. Herrick

Devon M. Herrick is a senior fellow at the National Center for Policy Analysis. He is an expert on twenty-first century medicine, including the evolution of Internet-based medicine and consumer-driven health care.

Most health plans provide some prescription drug benefits. Drug coverage is expected to increase as states expand Medicaid eligibility and millions of Americans obtain health insurance due to the Affordable Care Act.

Americans filled an estimated 3.8 billion retail prescriptions in 2011—about 12 per person in the United States, on average. Sixty percent of all Americans take a prescription drug in any given year, and nearly all seniors do. Drug therapy is arguably the most efficient method to treat most illnesses—often substituting for more expensive hospital and surgical treatments. Compared to other therapies, drugs are a relative bargain—but they can be expensive. Efforts to rein in the runaway cost of health care must focus on appropriate, but efficiently-administered, use of prescription drugs.

Specialized firms called pharmacy benefit managers (PBMs) help plan sponsors design and manage drug benefits, including which drugs are covered and which pharmacies participate in the drug plan. Regardless of how a program is structured, enrollees initially purchase most of their drugs at local pharmacies, which are reimbursed for the cost by the drug plans.

As drug coverage has become more widespread, so too have calls to impose additional regulations on drug plans and the firms managing them. A reason sometimes given for increasing drug plan regulation is the need for transparency to prevent drug plan managers from excessive mark-ups for drugs at the expense of patients and health plans. In the guise of protecting consumers, there are frequent calls for state and federal lawmakers to enact laws that hamper the efficient management of prescription drug benefits.

For instance, Mississippi transferred regulatory authority over drug plans from the state's insurance commissioner to the Board of Pharmacy. A similar initiative failed in Oregon. These efforts are short-sighted and unnecessary. Because state pharmacy boards are controlled by pharmacists, giving them authority over drug plans creates conflicts of interest that could undermine drug plans' ability to negotiate lower prices with pharmacy networks.

Regulations Result in Higher Drug Prices

Barriers to Efficient Networks. Drug plans are increasingly experimenting with limited or "narrow" pharmacy networks in order to lower drug prices through bargaining with specific drug dispensers. In return for exclusive access to enrollees, a smaller number of pharmacies compete to become network drug providers. But these networks sometimes run afoul of state laws that allow any pharmacy willing to abide by the terms of the contract to fill prescriptions for enrollees. These any-willing-pharmacy laws are costly to taxpayers, employers and patients alike. The Federal Trade Commission notes that these laws reduce the drug plans' bargaining power, leading to higher drug prices and higher premiums for consumers.

Barriers to Mail-Order Pharmacies. Drug plans use a variety of incentives to encourage patients to use efficient mail-order pharmacies for medications treating chronic conditions. Plan sponsors often charge higher deductibles for retail purchases or offer lower copayments for mail-order drugs. Some plans limit the number of times a prescription may be refilled at a retail pharmacy.

When the [Medicaid dispensing] fees are set too high, taxpayers pay pharmacies more than they would in a competitive market.

Unfortunately, some states are enacting laws that interfere with the ability of drug plans to reward enrollees that use the plan's mail order option by barring drug plans from offering lower prices for mail-order dispensing. This unnecessarily raises costs for consumers, insurers and employers. Obviously, these laws mostly aim to benefit local community pharmacies rather than consumers.

Barriers to Cost-Effective Formularies. Numerous drug therapies are available to treat most conditions, but some cost more than others. Thus it makes sense for drug plan sponsors to determine which drug therapies are included in a formulary. Though somewhat controversial in the past, formularies that exclude, substitute or discourage certain drugs are now commonplace in state Medicaid programs, Medicare Part D plans and employer plans. Patients (and their doctors) occasionally complain that drug plans substitute cheaper drugs (or generics) for expensive drugs prescribed by doctors. Claims of unauthorized drug substitution are rare, and most of them are ultimately determined to be unfounded.

Barriers to Lower Cost Dispensing Fees. Consumers who are not in a drug plan do not pay a separate dispensing fee when purchasing drugs. The costs of dispensing a drug—counting tablets, filling bottles and administrative tasks—are included in the retail cost. By contrast, dispensing fees in state-managed, conventional Medicaid plans are set by the state. State officials and state legislatures often yield to political pressure and set dispensing fees that are much higher than what private drugs plans could negotiate if allowed to do so. Consider, average Medicaid dispensing fees range from $1.75 in New Hampshire to $10.64 in Alabama, averaging about $4.22 per prescription across the country. By contrast, privately managed Medicare Part D plans negotiate fees with pharmacies of about $2 per prescription.

When the fees are set too high, taxpayers pay pharmacies more than they would in a competitive market.

Congress and state legislatures should avoid well-meaning, but ill-conceived, regulations intended to protect consumers, which often have the opposite result.

Barriers to Efforts to Combat Fraud. Health care fraud is a problem faced by all third party payers—drug plans are no exception. Estimates vary, but about 10 percent of Medicare claims could be either fraudulent or abusive, bordering on fraud. Concealed among the billions of claims filed electronically, fraudulent charges often look just like legitimate claims.

Companies that process electronic payments have learned how to detect transaction patterns that deviate from the norm. Computer algorithms can examine thousands of medical claims for services or medications for obvious irregularities. Sometimes a pattern emerges well after a series of fraudulent claims are processed and paid. Regulations requiring Medicare drug plan administrators to pay claims within 14 days make it difficult to detect fraud before a claim has been paid. At the very least, drug plans need the authority to delay paying questionable claims to providers suspected of fraud. Plans also need greater authority to exclude or suspend suspected fraudulent providers from networks and conduct routine audits of participating pharmacies.

Congress and state legislatures should avoid well-meaning, but ill-conceived, regulations intended to protect consumers, which often have the opposite result. A better way to ensure desirable outcomes is to promote a competitive environment free of market distortions that favor one party over another.

The goal of policymakers should be to allow competitive bidding among drug plan stakeholders in an environment free of perverse regulations that unduly advantage one party over another. Ultimately, society is better off when prices, profitability and services delivered are determined through this competitive process.

New Drugs Cost So Much to Develop That Pharmaceutical Companies Make Little Profit

Derek Lowe

Derek Lowe is an organic chemist who has worked for several major pharmaceutical companies on drug discovery projects.

Matthew Herper at *Forbes* has a very interesting column, building on some data from [biomedical consultant] Bernard Munos (whose work on drug development will be familiar to readers of this blog). What he and his colleague Scott DeCarlo have done is conceptually simple: they've gone back over the last 15 years of financial statements from a bunch of major drug companies, and they've looked at how many drugs each company has gotten approved.

Over that long a span, things should even out a bit. There will be some spending which won't show up in the count, that took place on drugs that got approved during the earlier part of that span, but (on the back end) there's spending on drugs in there that haven't made it to market yet, too. What do the numbers look like? Hideous. Appalling. Unsustainable.

AstraZeneca, for example, got 5 drugs on the market during this time span, the worst performance on this list, and thus spent nearly *$12 billion dollars per drug*. No wonder they're in the shape they're in. GSK, Sanofi, Roche, and Pfizer all spent in the range of $8 billion per approved drug. Amgen did things the cheapest by this measure, 9 drugs approved at about $3.7 billion per drug.

Now, there are several things to keep in mind about these numbers. First—and I know that I'm going to hear about this from some people—you might assume that different companies are putting different things under the banner of R&D [research and development] for accounting purposes. But there's a limit to how much of that you can do. Remember, there's a separate sales and marketing budget, too, of course, and people never get tired of pointing out that it's even larger than the R&D one. So how inflated can these figures be? Second, how can these numbers jibe with the 800-million-per-new-drug (recently revised to $1 billion), much less with the $43 million per new drug figure (from [researchers Donald W.] Light and [Rebecca] Warburton) that was making the rounds a few months ago [in 2011]?

Expenses [are] doing nothing but rising, and the success rate for drug discovery [is] going in the other direction.

Well, I tried to dispose of that last figure at the time. It's nonsense, and if it were true, people would be lining up to start drug companies (and other people would be throwing money at them to help). Meanwhile, the drug companies that already exist wouldn't be frantically firing thousands of people and selling their lab equipment at auction. Which they are. But what about that other estimate, the Tufts/diMasi [Tufts Center for the Study of Drug Development/Joseph A. DiMasi] one? What's the difference?

The Cost of Failure

As Herper rightly says, the biggest factor is failure. The Tufts estimate is for the costs racked up by one drug making it through. But looking at the whole R&D spend, you can see how money is being spent for all the stuff that *doesn't* get through. And as I and many of the other readers of this blog can testify, there's an awful lot of it. I'm now in my 23rd year of working in this industry, and nothing I've touched has ever made it to market yet. If someone wins $500 from a dollar slot machine, the proper way to figure the costs is to see how many dollars, total, they had to pump into the thing before they won—not just to figure that they spent $1 to win. (Unless, of course, they just sat down, and in this business we don't exactly have that option).

No, these figures really show you why the drug business is in the shape it's in. Look at those numbers, and look at how much a successful drug brings in, and you can see that these things don't always do a very good job of adding up. That's with the expenses doing nothing but rising, and the success rate for drug discovery going in the other direction, too. No one should be surprised that drug prices are rising under these conditions. The surprise is that there are still people out there trying to discover drugs.

Obamacare vs. Drug Innovation

William S. Smith

William S. Smith was formerly vice president for US public affairs and policy at Pfizer, Inc. He is currently managing director at NSI, a DC-based consulting firm.

With the release of the president's budget, it is now beyond dispute—Beltway spin notwithstanding—that the decision by the Pharmaceutical Research and Manufacturers of America (PhRMA) to support the health-care bill was one of the worst self-inflicted wounds in the history of lobbying. For biotech and pharmaceutical companies, the president's budget repudiates one of the most important benefits of their "deal" with the White House: the ability to market biotech drugs without generic competition for twelve years. The president would reduce that period to seven years, precisely the position of the generics industry and a position that the pharmaceutical industry had fought aggressively before it decided to make a deal with the president.

This embarrassing repudiation of the deal follows another hostile act from the Obama administration. On February 3, health and human services secretary Kathleen Sebelius released a letter to all the governors encouraging them to modify their states' Medicaid rules so as to use more generic drugs and to make deeper price cuts for drugs purchased in Medicaid. Since the industry had already agreed, when it signed onto the health-care bill, to cut deeply their prices for Medicaid drugs, Sebelius's inclusion of this advice in her letter to the governors was a gratuitous slap.

In fact, the best thing that could happen to the industry—and therefore to all those individuals, here and around the world, who benefit from the strides it has taken in research—would be an unraveling of PhRMA's deal. Since the president has walked away from the deal, now is the moment for the industry to walk away from a law that will significantly weaken the all-important U.S. market for pharmaceuticals.

Obamacare inflicts a series of balance-sheet hits on pharmaceutical companies

---

What will Obamacare do to America's premier health-care research industry?

First, Obamacare inflicts a series of balance-sheet hits on pharmaceutical companies. Last year, companies scrambled to write large rebate checks to satisfy the new price controls that the law imposed in the Medicaid program. In total, the price-control provisions of Obamacare will cost the industry $38 billion over the next ten years. During 2011, pharmaceutical companies will again be required to take out their checkbooks to pay a new $2.5 billion excise tax for this year, a tax that will grow to over $4 billion by 2018; this will cost the industry another $23 billion. Also, every January 1 the drug companies will be required to provide a 50 percent price discount for seniors who have reached the "doughnut hole" (i.e., the coverage gap in Medicare Part D); this represents about $30 billion in industry revenue that will need to be recovered elsewhere.

While these hits to the balance sheet will undoubtedly weaken the industry, cost U.S. jobs, and hinder further research, Beltway lobbyists persuaded Wall Street analysts that the industry "got off easy" because these extortion payments allowed it to fend off more serious congressional threats such as imposing price controls in Medicare and permitting unrestricted drug importation.

But the lobbyists missed the forest for the trees. These taxes and fees are less important than the implications of the law's gargantuan reordering of the pharmaceutical marketplace. Over the long term, Obamacare will cause a significant degradation of the private-sector market for pharmaceuticals, a market that has been the best in the world.

In the United States, 150 million citizens get their prescription drugs through their health insurance rather than directly from the government. Employers (and unions) contract with private health insurers to deliver the drug benefit, and the insurers negotiate with the pharmaceutical companies to decide which drugs they will cover and at what price.

Employees and retirees generally want access to the newest and best medicines, and their companies want to keep them happy and healthy. Therefore, the health plans serving employers do their best to balance cost with the need to provide high-quality medications.

Thus, the U.S. employer-provided insurance market offers the primary feature that drug companies need: a market that has incentives to reimburse for new medicines.

When Medicare Part D was created, Congress attempted, with some success, to re-create these market forces for seniors through a government-financed, but privately managed, health benefit. Under Part D, if a plan doesn't cover the particular drugs that a senior may want, he can sign up for another plan. Seniors will seek out new medicines that work, and so plans have reason to provide them.

Medicaid has the worst pricing structure and the worst track record in paying for innovations of any sector in the United States market.

Combined, employer-based and Part D health plans account for over 70 percent of the U.S. market for pharmaceuticals, meaning that the overwhelming majority of the U.S.

market is a healthy one, where prices are established by buyers and sellers negotiating innovation versus cost.

Obamacare would undermine this market by creating considerable incentives for employers to drop coverage for both employees and retirees. Douglas Holtz-Eakin, former director of the Congressional Budget Office, has estimated that the employer segment of the market may lose 35 million customers. The law also rescinds a tax deduction for employers who provide drug coverage to their retirees. Even those private-sector employees who keep their coverage will see their pharmaceutical benefits degraded as so-called "Cadillac plans"—the plans with the best pharmaceutical coverage—will take a huge 40 percent tax hit, giving employers significant cause to scale back drug benefits.

The law also contains two provisions that will weaken the market features of the Part D program: a Medicare payment commission that has the authority to set prices, and an "evidence-based" research institute that will tell Medicare patients (and everyone else) that they do not need all these new drugs.

While the healthy part of the pharmaceutical market will be pounded, the government-run segment of the market, Medicaid, will be expanded by 16 million patients. Medicaid has the worst pricing structure and the worst track record in paying for innovations of any sector in the United States market. Like government health-care systems around the world, Medicaid must be dragged to pay for medical advances. Unlike employers and seniors in Part D, Medicaid patients cannot vote with their feet if their health plan does not provide the new medicines they want. The incentives in Medicaid all run against paying for pharmaceutical innovations.

So, Obamacare significantly expands the worst sectors of the pharmaceutical market while degrading the best.

Despite these body blows to the pharmaceutical marketplace, Beltway business "experts" provide soothing reassurance that there will be "so many new customers" that no one should worry about the health of the industry. These new customers will appear in the so-called state exchanges that are slated to cover tens of millions of the currently uninsured. In fact, the exchanges are a market that does not yet exist and, one can surmise, will be a bad market for pharmaceuticals. Because of adverse selection and costly subsidies for lower-income par-ticipants, these exchanges will be plagued with cost overruns, as the Massachusetts exchange program currently is. Such a fiscal train wreck can only portend a market where pharma-ceutical benefits are lousy, prices are controlled, and innova-tion is not rewarded. Many of the Medicaid bureaucrats who currently impose price controls are the very people designing the state exchanges.

So, in exchange for a Beltway "win," PhRMA agreed to re-structure the entire U.S. pharmaceutical marketplace, to its considerable disadvantage. U.S. pharmaceutical companies al-ready face huge legal, scientific, and regulatory challenges and have shed more than 100,000 jobs in the last two years. PhRMA committed lobbying malpractice by agreeing to the Obamacare deal.

How did this happen? At the time the deal was struck, PhRMA was headed by a wheeler-dealer former congressman from Louisiana, Billy Tauzin, who was unfamiliar with the pharmaceutical business. Most of the CEOs of individual companies who might have stood up to Tauzin were either Democrats eager to please the administration, or Europeans without a sound footing in American politics.

It is not too late. The 2010 election, new leadership of PhRMA, and the movement to repeal Obamacare had already offered hope that the worst might be avoided. Now that the president has repudiated a central pillar of the deal, the indus-try is free to support a wholesale repeal of the law, not through clever back-room deals or partisan maneuvering, but through an open declaration that drug innovation is at stake. The pharmaceutical industry will never be popular, but if Beltway dealmaking replaces innovation, it will simultaneously court public opprobrium and commercial disaster.

CHAPTER 3

How Serious Is the Problem of Prescription Drug Abuse?

Chapter Preface

Prescription drug abuse is the fastest growing drug problem in the United States. More people now die from unintentional drug overdoses than from traffic accidents, and according to the Centers for Disease Control and Prevention (CDC), since 2003, more of these deaths have involved prescription painkillers than heroin and cocaine combined. Statistically, for every death, thirty-five people visit emergency departments, 161 report drug abuse or dependence, and 461 report nonmedical uses of painkillers that are legally available only by prescription. In a 2009 survey, roughly five million people admitted to having used them nonmedically in the past month.

Some of these users obtain the pills from their own doctors and become dependent on them after their pain is gone. Others "doctor shop" and obtain duplicate prescriptions from several doctors. But many more get them from friends or relatives, buy them on the street, or simply steal them. Sometimes they steal from patients who need them to control severe pain. And some teens steal pills from their parents' medicine cabinets without realizing how dangerous it is to take drugs that have been prescribed for someone else.

Many people, including many parents, are simply unaware of the danger. They mistakenly assume that because a drug has been approved by the government and is given by doctors, it must be safe—or at least safer than illegal drugs. But this is not the case. Many experts believe that prescription drugs present an even greater danger to society than illegal drugs because they cannot be banned entirely and no harm is expected by those who take them illicitly.

There is no such thing as a drug that cannot cause harm. All drugs have multiple effects; the ones unrelated to the purpose for which they are prescribed are called "side effects," but these effects are not necessarily minor. Many side effects can damage the body; some can even cause death. When a doctor prescribes a drug, he or she has to judge whether for that particular patient, the expected benefit is greater than the risk. When a person is seriously ill, it often is. Whether risks are justified in dealing with less serious conditions is controversial even among doctors. Everyone agrees, however, that prescription drugs can be harmful to people who do not have the condition they are designed to treat, or who also have other conditions that would cause the drug to interact in a damaging way. Not all bodies are alike, and even if a specific drug helps one person, it may hurt others.

Moreover, just because a person does not have an immediate bad reaction to a drug does not mean that no harm has been done. Many of the effects of prescription drugs are slow and cumulative. For this reason, doctors monitor patients who are taking powerful drugs to determine what effects they are having. Adverse effects may show up years later, producing a different illness, perhaps even a worse one, on top of the disease the person started with. Such risks cannot be avoided when someone is ill enough to need treatment. It is tragic, however, when people who are not sick incur them by taking drugs without medical supervision.

Although all prescription drugs carry risks—which is why they were placed in the "prescription" category in the first place—painkillers are the ones most commonly abused. They are a great blessing to cancer patients and others who are in severe pain. It cannot be said that the public would be better off if they did not exist. Yet as illegal use of them grows, more and more restrictions are placed on doctors' right to prescribe them, thus making them harder for people who actually need them to get—something abusers do not think about when they assume that their actions affect only themselves. Some doctors have become reluctant to prescribe such drugs for patients in pain lest they inadvertently give them to someone who is faking it.

Misuse of painkillers affects not only those injured by them, but countless innocent people and families. According to a December 2012 CNN report titled "Prescription Drugs 'Orphan' Children in Eastern Kentucky," more than eighty-six thousand Kentucky children are being raised by someone who is not their biological parent—in many cases because their parents have overdosed on prescription drugs. "The kids go from couch to couch and from home to home, living in a constant state of transience," states the report. "For those children whose parents have not overdosed but are deep in their addiction, there is a sense of perpetual wariness about what they might find when they get home from school."

"You're always worried ... if your parents are even going to be there, you know, what's going on in your house?" said Avery Bradshaw, a sixteen-year-old student at Rockcastle County High School who is being raised by great-grandparents because his father overdosed on Oxycontin when he was seven. "A lot of kids have to go through that every day and it definitely wears them down, you know."

Government authorities are deeply concerned about prescription drug abuse and are making detailed plans to combat it. But no effort to reduce the harm it causes can be successful unless people realize that taking drugs not prescribed for them is hazardous.

Many People Are Addicted to Drugs That Were Prescribed for Them in the Past

Randy Turner

Randy Turner is a reporter for the Winnipeg Free Press *in Canada.*

The absolute worst thing, Jerry admitted, was stealing pain-killers from the terminally ill.

He lived in a small town in southern Manitoba [Canada], so it wasn't hard to find a cancer patient. He'd scope their house, like a thief, and wait for them to leave—if they could.

"It's very sick and twisted," the 29-year-old confessed.

Wait. You'd steal drugs from people who were dying? Who needed that medication to ease their pain?

Jerry didn't blink. "No problem," he said. "There's no end to what you'll do as an addict. The things I've done . . . it's crazy."

Jerry isn't a common thief. At least, he wasn't until undergoing hip surgery a few years back. Doctors gave him Percocet at first, and it worked like a seducing charm. Soon he was gobbling hydromorphone pills.

"It was a better buzz," he said.

His doctor got wise to Jerry's addiction and refused to up his dosage. Didn't matter. Jerry adapted, finding friends or acquaintances—or even strangers he'd met in a bar—and piggyback off their prescriptions.

In desperate times, he'd stalk delivery trucks parked in front of pharmacies. Thirty seconds, in and out. He'd shake the boxes and grab the ones that "sounded like pills."

"Eventually, the drugs took over my life," he said. "I was pretty much a walking dead for three years."

Jerry represents the changing face of addiction in North America. He also symbolizes the dark side of a society that is gobbling up prescription drugs at what many experts believe are alarming rates.

Painkillers. Antidepressants. Anti-anxiety medications. Sleeping pills. Sedatives.

Pills, pills, pills. All are addictive. If abused and mixed together, or combined with alcohol, they can be lethal.

Readily Available Drugs

Welcome to the 21st century, where mood-altering drugs no longer need to be procured through illegal transactions in back alleys. You don't need a dealer. You need a doctor. And most of these medications—unlike cocaine and marijuana—are not only readily available from your friendly professional, white-coated pharmacist, but marketed through TV ads streaming into Canada from the United States, where the proliferation of prescription-drug misuse is No. 1 with a tablet.

This is not about OxyContin addiction on Main Street. This is about everyday folks trying to get by on less.

Teachers dealing with stress.

A college student fretting about finals.

A workaholic trying to get a good night's sleep.

Or a construction worker dealing with chronic pain just to make it through another shift.

"This type of abuse is not something we've seen before," said Deborah Cumming, national priority adviser at the Canadian Centre on Substance Abuse in Ottawa. "It's really changing how we understand what substance abuse and misuse is. It's pervasive across all social classes and all demographics.

"People are usually associating substance abusers or people with addiction issues as someone using a dirty needle on the street, using heroin. This is very different because the sources are therapeutically legitimate medications coming through the health system, for the most part.

"And we still need these medications to treat chronic and acute pain. That just complicates things even further."

Just ask the health professionals on the front lines, the pharmacists, who over the last decade have seen the prescriptions for painkillers, sleeping pills and pills for anxiety and stress fly across their counters.

"Definitely, you'd be surprised," replied Christian Onyebuchi, a pharmacist from Transcona, when asked if the number of such prescriptions has risen noticeably over the last decade.

"You go into the doctor's office now and say you're tired or feeling down, and they'll prescribe an antidepressant for you. Doctors have pills for every little thing.

"People just can't handle stress anymore. People want things as easy as possible. The world is changing."

There is no magical fix for prescription-drug misuse, a complex, multi-dimensional issue.

Another young pharmacist working at a large chain didn't want to be named but said, "I'm surprised, being a new grad, just how many people take these drugs. I knew people took them. I just didn't know there were that many."

Thomas Ling, who runs his own pharmacy on Henderson Highway, cites societal changes such as an aging population and economic stress. And notably the invasion of television ads for pharmaceutical drugs from the U.S. that stream across the border as easily as episodes of the *Big Bang Theory* [television show].

"They give you the impression (prescription drugs) are a magical fix," Ling said.

No Magical Fix

Ironically, there is no magical fix for prescription-drug misuse, a complex, multi-dimensional issue that is now beginning to manifest itself in a range of unsettling consequences from the worst (death) to the dangerous (kids stealing prescription drugs from their parents' medicine cabinets) to the desperate (stealing pain medication from the terminally ill). . . .

"Imagine a world where we didn't have access to painkillers?," offered Susan Ulan, senior medical adviser to the College of Physicians in Alberta and co-chairwoman of the province's Coalition on Prescription Drug Misuse.

"It doesn't mean we stop prescribing those medications just because a small number of people can run into problems with it. It's all about balance."

Prescription-drug abuse now accounts for more overdoses than heroin and cocaine combined.

As a family physician, however, Ulan sees first-hand the increasing tendency for patients suffering from pain, stress, anxiety or sleep disorders to seek medication in the form of prescription drugs.

"From a human-nature point of view, it's easier for a person to take a tablet than actually make lifestyle changes," she noted. "Because lifestyle changes take a lot more effort. It's human nature to find the quickest, easiest way to solve a problem. But that doesn't work very well when you're dealing with chronic pain or addiction.". . .

Just last week [May 2012], the U.S. government reported for the first time in the county's history the No. 1 cause of accidental deaths was prescription drugs—eclipsing car accidents and gunshots.

Prescription-drug abuse now accounts for more overdoses than heroin and cocaine combined, according to the U.S. Centers for Disease Control and Prevention. Of the 37,000 people who died of a drug overdose in 2009, roughly 40 per cent—more than 15,000—were using prescription opiates.

In 2000, American retail pharmacies dispensed 174 million prescriptions for opiates; by 2009 that figure had climbed to 257 million, an increase of 48 per cent in less than a decade. . . .

Last year, 63 per cent of people on prescription drugs strayed from doctor's orders or sought out pills that weren't intended for them at all.

Hidden Medication

Many people who prescribe to antidepressants or anti-anxiety medications, or sleeping pills or painkillers, don't advertise their prescription-drug use. Not even to their family doctor.

In fact, in a recent U.S. study that involved the analysis of 76,000 urine samples submitted last year [2011], 63 per cent of people on prescription drugs strayed from doctor's orders or sought out pills that weren't intended for them at all. The Quest Diagnostics study found most of the drugs found were painkillers, sedatives or amphetamines.

Translation: Patients will hide their real prescription-drug use even from their own family doctor. . . .

Teen Challenge executive director Steve Paulson will display the cabinet containing prescription medications for many of the rehabilitation centre's 30 "students."

"Almost everybody who comes in here is on some sort of feel-good drug," Paulson said. "Something to have them deal with their anxiety. It's so over-prescribed. (The pills) are so easy to get. This is the society we live in. It's off the chain right now."

Take Mark, 21, who has been at Teen Challenge going on 18 months. His mother was a nurse who became hooked on painkillers when he was a baby. She weighed 95 pounds when she died. Mark was seven years old and vowed never to touch drugs.

As a teenager, he was introduced first to marijuana, then Percocet, which he acquired from a friend, who got them from his mother. "She actually gave them to him to sell," Mark said.

Most health-care experts agree the spike in the sale of anti-anxiety and antidepressant medications in particular can be linked directly to the increase in recent years in television advertising.

Within a few months, Mark was addicted. What resulted was an endless string of con jobs, fraud and theft—anything to get drugs. While still in school, Mark and his friends would crush up Percocet pills and smoke weed. They'd get their hands on fentanyl patches, used to treat arthritis and joint pain, cut them into squares, heat them over tinfoil and smoke them like crack.

Mark doesn't believe he's alone.

"People," he said, "are taking lorazepam like it's candy," he noted, referring to the prescription drug "in the Valium family." . . .

Disease Mongering

Most health-care experts agree the spike in the sale of anti-anxiety and antidepressant medications in particular can be linked directly to the increase in recent years in television advertising that largely features happy people skipping through flowery fields and ends with, "Consult your doctor" and a quickly spouted list of potential side-effects.

It's the pharmaceutical industry's collective answer to "We've got an app for that."

Dr. Joel Lexchin, from the School of Health Policy and Management at York University in Toronto, says there's a phrase for such direct-to-consumer marketing: disease mongering.

The concept is based on mass marketing. For example, Lexchin said most antidepressants wouldn't reap significant profits if they were simply sold to people with a serious condition.

"But there are a lot more people with mild depression than serious depression," he noted. "So drug companies market to people with mild depression because there's a lot more money to be made.

"The drug companies can't do this on their own," Lexchin added. "To some extent, they're feeding off what goes on in the rest of the world. There's economic stress. Factories are closing. People are worried about their jobs. The drug companies are picking up on that."

The average American is subjected to 14 prescription-drug ads a day.

Another example: A drug called Paxil hit the open market to treat major depression in 1992. Now it's prescribed for everything from obsessive compulsive disorder to what's termed social anxiety, the latter a condition that used to go by another common term.

"Prior to this, we just called it shyness," said Alan Cassels, a drug policy researcher at the University of Victoria and co-author of *Selling Sickness: How the Biggest Pharmaceutical Companies Are Turning Us All into Patients.*

"That's a classic case of the drug market basically pushing the creation of the disease. So you saw full-page ads and television advertisements for this condition that was said to affect millions of people. They had questionnaires that said, 'Do you like speaking in public?' I mean, most people don't. Or 'Do you sometimes feel nervous at meetings or other social gatherings?' Of course, a lot of people do. That doesn't mean they're ill."

Cassels' research revealed the average American is subjected to 14 prescription-drug ads a day. Canadians, via U.S. television feeds, are exposed to a similar extent.

"My question is, what does that do to the psychological health of the population when you are essentially telling people several times an hour that they could be sick and they need help?" Cassels asked.

Short answer: You push a lot of pharmaceuticals. . . .

Added Cassels: "Here's the big problem, in my opinion: Both consumers and physicians are too easily seduced by the promise of a quick fix. That's not to say the drugs don't work in some people because clearly they do. But does everyone who's in a little bit of pain need an opioid? Or does everyone who's experienced some bouts of shyness need an antidepressant called Paxil?

"At one level, it just reflects the crazy society we live in, where we just expect instant food, instant gratification and instant health-care solutions."

No Single Group to Blame

So it's society's fault, right? Or those unscrupulous drug companies? Or too many doctors willing to write a prescription and move along to the next patient?

[Professor Benedikt] Fischer [director of the Simon Fraser University Centre for Applied Research in Mental Health and Addiction], for one, doesn't blame the drug makers.

"I'm by no means a defender of the pharmaceutical industry, but that's not the pharmaceutical industry's job," he said. "They are businesses, and they're interested in selling and disseminating as much of their product as they can. The onus here is on the state and governments to properly regulate these drugs. That's a bit like blaming the tobacco industry for the quantity of tobacco use."

But what about the responsibility of patients looking for a quick fix rather than investing—in some cases—in the more laborious, time-consuming efforts of lifestyle change?

[Doctors] can't stop the endless and increasing volume of patients who are convinced the answer to all their problems—as seen on TV—is a little blue or green pill.

"Well, I agree to some extent," Fischer replied. "But the onus is on the professionals who provide these pills. Don't forget, you can't just walk in anywhere, to a 7-Eleven, and get these drugs. They're given to people by medical professionals, right? These are the gatekeepers. They're trained, they're paid to give the best medical practice they can.

"They (doctors) are not in the business of harming people. But you have to understand a little of how the medical system works. Doctors are entrepreneurs. In many ways, prescribing a pill to a patient is the easiest and quickest way to deal with a patient's problem rather than going into more in-depth analysis or alternative interventions. It's almost an industrial medical system we've created here.

"The doctor on average has three to five minutes with a patient who comes in and says, 'Oh, my back hurts' or 'I'm feeling stressed out.' Taking the prescription pad and writing a script for a drug that will cure the symptoms for a while is often the easiest and most efficient thing to do, unfortunately. Whether it's the right thing to do is a totally different question."

Still, doctors can't stop patients from lying to them. They can't stop addicts from robbing delivery trucks. They can't stop the endless and increasing volume of patients who are convinced the answer to all their problems—as seen on TV—is a little blue or green pill.

"There's no single person or company to blame," Lexchin said. "Everybody has some responsibility in this."

But if the target for blame is not easily identifiable, those who ultimately pay the price for abuse and misuse are identifiable, Lexchin concluded.

"It's dangerous because all drugs have side-effects," he said. "And the reason we take them is because we think the benefits will outweigh the risks. But the milder your condition, the less likely you're going to get any benefit of the drug, but you still have the same risk of having harm."

So what's the prescription? Increasingly, people are dying from misusing legal drugs. An addict is born every day.

Yet pharmaceutical companies are going to keep pushing the next feel-good pill. Doctors won't get any less pressure to prescribe. And the next batch of anxiety-ridden, sleep-deprived, painkiller-seeking consumers will be waiting.

At this rate, all the hydromorphone in North America won't stop the health-care system or law enforcement or society in general from feeling the pain. No quick fixes, either.

"It's a bit of a perfect storm," Cumming said. "We really need to have a comprehensive approach. We've got gaps in all these streams, and we need to start working together. Everybody has a role to play. This is a game-changer for everybody involved.

"Because it's so complex you can't expect just one silver bullet for this. That is the worst thing anyone can expect."

One in Four Teens Admits to Having Misused or Abused a Prescription Drug

Cassie Goldberg

Cassie Goldberg is Assistant Director, Public Affairs and Digital Communicationds for the Partnership at Drugfree.org.

New, nationally projectable survey results released today [April 2013] by The Partnership at Drugfree.org and MetLife Foundation confirmed that one in four teens has misused or abused a prescription (Rx) drug at least once in their lifetime—a 33 percent increase over the past five years. The Partnership Attitude Tracking Study (PATS) also found troubling data on teen misuse or abuse of prescription stimulants. One in eight teens (13 percent) now reports that they have taken the stimulants Ritalin or Adderall when it was not prescribed for them, at least once in their lifetime.

Contributing to this sustained trend in teen medicine abuse are the lax attitudes and beliefs of parents and caregivers. In fact, nearly one-third of parents say they believe Rx stimulants like Ritalin or Adderall, normally prescribed for attention deficit hyperactivity disorder (ADHD), can improve a teen's academic performance even if the teen does not have ADHD. Parents are not effectively communicating the dangers of Rx medicine misuse and abuse to their kids, nor are they safeguarding their medications at home and disposing of unused medications properly.

Concerning Trends in Teen Prescription Drug Abuse

The new PATS data confirm that misuse and abuse of prescription drugs is now a normalized behavior among teens:

- One in four teens (24 percent) reports having misused or abused a prescription drug at least once in their lifetime (up from 18 percent in 2008 to 24 percent in 2012), which translates to about 5 million teens. That is a 33 percent increase over a five-year period.

- Almost one in four teens (23 percent) say their parents don't care as much if they are caught using Rx drugs without a doctor's prescription, compared to getting caught with illegal drugs.

- Of those kids who said they abused Rx medications, one in five (20 percent) has done so before age 14.

- More than a quarter of teens (27 percent) mistakenly believe that misusing and abusing prescription drugs is safer than using street drugs.

- One-third of teens (33 percent) say they believe "it's okay to use prescription drugs that were not prescribed to them to deal with an injury, illness or physical pain."

"These data make it very clear: the problem is real, the threat immediate and the situation is not poised to get better," said Steve Pasierb, President and CEO [chief executive officer] of The Partnership at Drugfree.org. "Parents fear drugs like cocaine or heroin and want to protect their kids. But the truth is that when misused and abused, medicines—especially stimulants and opioids—can be every bit as dangerous and harmful as those illicit street drugs. Medicine abuse is one of the most significant and preventable adolescent health problems facing our families today. What's worse is that kids who begin using at an early age are more likely to struggle with substance use disorders when compared to those who might start using after the teenage years. As parents and caring adults, we need to take definitive action to address the risks that intentional medicine abuse poses to the lives and the long-term health of our teens."

Significant Increase in Teen Abuse of Stimulants Ritalin and Adderall

Rx stimulants are a key area of concern, with misuse and abuse of Ritalin and Adderall in particular driving the noted increases in teen medicine abuse. Stimulants are a class of drugs that enhance brain activity and are commonly prescribed to treat health conditions including ADHD and obesity. The 2012 data found:

- One in eight teens (about 2.7 million) now reports having misused or abused the Rx stimulants Ritalin or Adderall at least once in their lifetime.

- 9 percent of teens (about 1.9 million) report having misused or abused the Rx stimulants Ritalin or Adderall in the past year (up from 6 percent in 2008) and 6 percent of teens (1.3 million) report abuse of Ritalin or Adderall in the past month (up from 4 percent in 2008).

- One in four teens (26 percent) believes that prescription drugs can be used as a study aid.

"We need to make sure that children and adolescents receive a thorough assessment before being placed on stimulant medications, and that if medication is prescribed to a child, it should only be as one component of a comprehensive ADHD management plan," said Alain Joffe, MD, MPH, Director, Student Health and Wellness Center at Johns Hopkins University and Former Chairman, American Academy of Pediatrics Committee on Substance Abuse. "We don't really know what long-term effects these ADHD medications will have on the still-developing brains of adolescents who do not have ADHD. We do know they can have significant side effects, which is why they are limited to use with a prescription."

> *More than four in 10 teens ... who have misused or abused a prescription drug obtained it from their parent's medicine cabinet.*

Abuse of prescription pain medicine remains at unacceptably high levels among teens, but the new PATS data show it may be flattening. Teen abuse of prescription pain relievers like Vicodin and OxyContin has remained stable since 2011, with one in six teens (16 percent) reporting abuse or misuse of an Rx pain reliever at least once in their lifetime and one in 10 teens (10 percent) admitting to abusing or misusing an Rx painkiller in the past year.

Lax Attitudes and Permissiveness About Rx Drugs

Parent permissiveness and lax attitudes toward abuse and misuse of Rx medicines, coupled with teens' ease of access to prescription medicines in the home, are key factors linked to teen medicine misuse and abuse. The availability of prescription drugs (in the family medicine cabinet, in the homes of friends and family) makes them that much easier to abuse. The new survey findings stress that teens are more likely to abuse Rx medicines if they think their parents "don't care as much if they get caught using prescription drugs, without a doctor's prescription, than they do if they get caught using illegal drugs."

- Almost one-third of parents (29 percent) say they believe ADHD medication can improve a child's academic or testing performance, even if the teen does not have ADHD.

- One in six parents (16 percent) believes that using prescription drugs to get high is safer than using street drugs.

- Teens reported that during the last conversation they had with their parents regarding substance abuse, only 16 percent said they discussed the misuse or abuse of prescription pain relievers with their parents, and just 14 percent indicate the same for discussions about any type of prescription drug. In comparison, a majority of teens (81 percent) say they have discussed the risks of marijuana use with their parents, 80 percent have discussed alcohol and nearly one-third of teens (30 percent) have discussed crack/cocaine.

- More than half of teens (56 percent) indicate that it's easy to get prescription drugs from their parent's medicine cabinet. In fact, about half of parents (49 percent) say anyone can access their medicine cabinet.

- More than four in 10 teens (42 percent) who have misused or abused a prescription drug obtained it from their parent's medicine cabinet. Almost half (49 percent) of teens who misuse or abuse Rx medicines obtained them from a friend.

Parents do not seem to be as concerned with prescription drug abuse as they are with use of illicit drugs.

Teens are more likely to use prescription drugs if they believe that their parents are more lenient toward prescription drug misuse or abuse compared to illegal drug abuse, and if their parents use drugs themselves.

- One in five parents (20 percent) report that they have given their teen a prescription drug that was not prescribed for them.

- The PATS survey also found that 17 percent of parents do not throw away expired medications, and 14 percent of parents say that they themselves have misused or abused prescription drugs within the past year.

Parents' Missed Opportunity

"This new data is not about blaming parents. Rather, it's an urgent call to action for them to use their immense power to help curb this dangerous behavior. It's about missed opportunities to protect their kids by having direct conversations with them about the health risks of misusing and abusing medicines—and to then moving to safeguard the medicines in their own home," said Pasierb. "Parental apathy on this issue is contributing to the problem. Yet the same data show year in and year out that kids who learn a lot about the risks of drug use at home are up to half as likely to use as kids who don't get that life-changing gift from their parents."

The 2012 PATS study also shows that parents do not seem to be as concerned with prescription drug abuse as they are with use of illicit drugs. A majority of parents (80 percent) are at least somewhat concerned about illicit drug abuse compared to 70 percent who report being concerned about Rx drug abuse. But in reality, teens are more likely to have abused prescription medicine within their lifetime more than many other substances, with 12 percent of teens abusing Ecstasy, nine percent abusing crack/cocaine and 15 percent abusing inhalants within their lifetime.

"Parents need to be very clear in the messages they send their kids about the misuse and abuse of prescription medications," said Dennis White, President and CEO of MetLife Foundation. "It is important for parents and caregivers to set a good example in their own families. This includes using their own medicines properly, safeguarding medications in their own homes and properly disposing of unused medicines so teens won't have easy access to them."

A New Prescription for Fighting Drug Abuse

Ron Schachter

Ron Schachter is a contributing writer to District Administration, *a magazine for school administrators.*

It's a drug prevention conversation—and program—that was largely missing as recently as a decade ago in most middle and high schools. In those days, the principal concern of health educators and disciplinarians alike was to keep students from misusing alcohol and illegal street drugs such as ecstasy, cocaine and even heroin.

But driven by the proliferation of high-powered prescription drugs, from the highly addictive painkiller OxyContin to the ADHD [attention deficit hyperactivity disorder] remedy Adderall—and sobered by prescription drug abuse statistics for school-age children—educational leaders are answering back with a host of new initiatives targeted to that very problem and aimed largely at middle schools, where such drug abuse often begins.

The statistics are daunting. According to a 2011 study funded by the MetLife Foundation, more than 3.2 million—1 in 4—high school students admitted to abusing prescription drugs at least once in their lives. In a 2008 survey by the White House Office of National Drug Control Policy, using prescription drugs illegally ranked second only to marijuana use among teens. Another government study in 2007 found that illicit prescription drugs were the drugs of choice for 12- and 13-year olds.

Besides the risk of addiction and overdoses, the widespread and unauthorized use of these drugs is having other far-reaching effects. The 2009 National Risk Behavior Survey conducted by the Centers for Disease Control [and Prevention] showed a strong correlation between illicit prescription drug use and academic performance in high school. Of those students who had taken such drugs once or more, 26 percent earned mostly Cs, while 41 percent registered Ds and Fs.

Last fall [2011], the National Association of School Nurses (NASN) started distributing "Smart Moves, Smart Choices," a comprehensive "school toolkit" designed to prevent prescription drug abuse and featuring noted authority [Dr.] Drew Pinsky in a series of video segments.

Besides the unprecedented abundance of such drugs, many teens think these substances are perfectly legal and safe.

"It was a data-driven decision," says NASN's director of government affairs, Mary Louise Embrey, of the new initiative. "Every day, 2,500 young people abuse prescription drugs for the first time."

The National Education Association's (NEA) Health Information Network is creating an anti-prescription-drug-abuse curriculum that its framers promise will adhere to the National Health Education Standards and to the Common Core State Standards. The curriculum is scheduled for release at the NEA's national conference in July [2012].

Some school districts, meanwhile, have taken prescription drug education into their own hands—the result, say their leaders, of growing abuse in their communities and fatalities in their schools.

A New Epidemic

The creators of the new programs say it's no surprise that the teenage abuse of prescription drugs has reached epidemic proportions. Besides the unprecedented abundance of such drugs, many teens think these substances are perfectly legal and safe. "They don't necessarily have the maturity level to understand that a drug—even if it comes from a doctor—may not be safe if it isn't used as prescribed," Embrey explains. "In the teenage mind, there's the perception that (abusing) the drug is not illegal because it comes from a doctor."

"Most kids would never consider doing heroin," adds Lisa Roberts, co-founder of the Scioto County Prescription Drug Abuse Task Force in southeastern Ohio, which has provided funding for surrounding school districts to create new programs. "A lot would consider taking a pill because it came from a doctor and must be safe. But the reality is that Oxy-Contin and hydrocodone (the generic form of OxyContin) will addict you. I know tons of kids who became addicted that way."

Parents—often without knowing it—have become the "dealers" of prescription drugs simply by leaving them unguarded in the medicine cabinet.

It doesn't help that some popular institutions take the misuse of prescription drugs lightly, adds Pamela Bennett, executive director of healthcare alliance development at the pharmaceutical company Purdue Pharma, which developed the widely distributed pain killer OxyContin and is funding the new NEA curriculum.

"There are symbols in our culture that make this [kind of drug abuse] appear to be more of a social norm than using methamphetamines and heroin," she observes.

Bennett recalls an episode of the television series *Will & Grace* in which one character kept a "party bowl" of prescription drugs, and she also notes that rapper Eminem wears a tattoo spelling out Vicodin, another powerful painkiller to which the singer was once addicted.

What complicates matters, adds Bennett and other advocates for prescription drug education, is that parents—often without knowing it—have become the "dealers" of prescription drugs simply by leaving them unguarded in the medicine cabinet. Most of the new anti-abuse programs include components to raise parental awareness and to promote the proper disposal of any unused medications.

More than a decade ago, a study of 11- to 18-year-old students with ADHD in Wisconsin and Minnesota revealed that 34 percent reported being approached to sell or trade their medicines, such as Ritalin. Since then, reports the National Institute of Mental Health, the number of youngsters and teens with prescription medications for ADHD has risen by more than 500,000, raising the specter of even more illicit sharing and selling.

Smart Moves, Smart Choices

The National Association of School Nurses made a splash last October when it released "Smart Moves, Smart Choices," which contains everything from guidelines on running school assemblies and finding local speakers to a flier that can be sent home to parents. The flier covers the statistics and risks of prescription drug abuse among teens, identifies the most commonly abused medications, and offers steps for securing such drugs at home and recognizing signs of abuse in children.

Colorful posters from the kit present snappy slogans such as "Small things can be deadly," along with pictures of an overturned bottle of pills next to a tarantula. The success of NASN's anti-abuse initiative is also riding on the video segments of Pinsky—better known through his television appearances as "Dr. Drew"—addressing a high school assembly at King-Drew High School in Los Angeles [California].

The segments run about five minutes long and are divided into topics with titles such as "What Is Addiction?" and "Why Kids Abuse." In the segment "Smart Moves For Teens," Dr.

Pinsky explains how to help peers involved with illicit prescription drugs. "Talk to your friends about the dangers of prescription drug abuse," Pinsky suggests. "Reach out to resources in your community; your school nurse is a perfect place to go—your teachers, guidance counselors, even your friend's parents. There is help. You could save your friend's life."

"He has the star power of a well-known professional in the world of substance abuse," says Embrey. "I was at the assembly where we filmed the videos, and I've never seen students so attentive. They were hanging on every word."

Embrey also points to the five video segments created with MacNeil/Lehrer Productions and included in "Smart Moves, Smart Choices." These videos cover areas such as the science of addiction, myths about prescription drug abuse—including the belief that these drugs are harmless and that abusers are immune from addiction—and testimonials by students who formerly abused.

"The combination of real students talking on this issue, along with Dr. Drew, make this a winner," Embrey says. NASN has distributed almost 4,000 of the kits and also offers their entire contents—minus the posters—online.

Dee Smith, the school nurse at Mountain Trail Middle School in Phoenix [Arizona], did not take long to order the kit—or to put it into action. A week after receiving it, Smith put on an hour-long assembly for about 150 of the school's 850 students. Besides holding additional assemblies for the remainder, Smith plans on spreading the prescription drug message over the school year by running individual videos during her school's morning announcements, which are broadcast through video monitors in each classroom.

"I love how the snippets are less than five minutes each," Smith notes. "And there are not many programs that focus on prescription drugs."

Smith hopes that the parental piece will have more success than past drug education initiatives. "I've had an auditorium reserved for 600 people and had fewer than 10 show up," she recalls. "There's a 'not my kid' mentality. When I call home suspecting a kid of using drugs, the parents deny it. If I offer them a free drug-testing kit, they don't come in to pick it up."

Building a Standards-Based Curriculum

The NEA also is developing free materials on prescription drug abuse and is integrating that subject into a broader approach to using prescription drugs properly throughout life. Nora Howley, NEA's manager of programs, is aiming to find a place in the middle school curriculum of standards-driven school systems.

"We're not aware of anything else like we're doing," Howley explains. "These materials will be tied to Common Core standards in health education and also to the reading standard of navigating and using nonfiction information."

Reading about the dangers of prescription drug abuse and the choices individuals can make, for instance, would align with that reading standard. The curriculum would also cover health education objectives from identifying personal behaviors that cause health risks to assisting others in avoiding such risks.

"Teachers can drop it into the curriculum and it will help them meet their standards," adds National Education Association President Jerald Newberry.

Howley says that the new curriculum, due out in July, focuses on grades 6–8 and will consist of life skills units that not only cover the abuse of prescription drugs but that teach students such lessons as not to take leftover medications for a future illness without a physician's guidance.

"We think its really important that students understand all of these life decisions. The idea is to have students set a behavioral goal around prescription drugs," Howley says. "Until now, most students would finish high school and not have one conversation about this subject."

The NEA will distribute 10,000 of the new curriculum packets, with an eye toward state and local health education coordinators, who would pass them on to health and science teachers in schools across the nation. The materials will also be available online. Both the NASN and NEA initiatives are funded by pharmaceutical companies—Janssen Pharmaceuticals in the case of "Smart Moves, Smart Choices" and Purdue Pharma for the forthcoming NEA materials.

Lessons from Experience

Some districts that have come face-to-face with prescription drug abuse and its consequences have embarked on prevention programs of their own. Mark Selle, the superintendent of the Chewalah and Valley School Districts in rural eastern Washington state, has witnessed no shortage of tragedies. In one case, a 12-year-old brought hydrocodone tablets to a slumber party. In another case, a 21-year-old former student died after smoking the contents of a Fentanyl patch, originally prescribed for pain management. And an eighth-grader had died from a methadone overdose.

"Kids were dying, suddenly, and so young," Selle says. "I knew a principal who had OxyContin prescribed after a skiing accident and became addicted. He stopped cold turkey but described to me the hell it was to break the addiction.

"In our little town of Chewalah, drugstores were getting held up all the time," says school counselor Loretta Kron. "And we said, 'Let's find some stakeholders and people as passionate as we are. Let's do something to help our small community.'"

The result was the creation in 2007 of the organization Prescriptions for Life. The effort was spearheaded by fourth-grade teacher Sherry Tilla and her husband, Jim, whose daughter Hayley first tried OxyContin in her sophomore year in high school and became addicted. Besides circulating a DVD telling her story, the parents make the rounds of schools as far as an hour away to speak with students in assemblies and classrooms and with teachers in staff development sessions.

Kron recalls the Tillas' first presentation at the Valley Elementary and Middle School four years ago. "A lot of kids had the attitude, 'That won't happen to me.' When the Tillas told their story, you could probably hear a pin drop. It was affecting a fourth-grade teacher whom these students knew."

Selle and other school leaders were active in advocating for a statewide prescription monitoring program, a shared database for pharmacies that keeps track of anyone receiving a prescription and prevents abusers from "pharmacy hopping" to get multiple prescriptions filled. The program started collecting data from pharmacies around the state last October [2011].

"It's essential that the schools be involved," Selle insists. "In terms of advocating for legislation, the voice of school personnel speaks loudly. We have the stories, and the more kids we can get speaking out the better."

Last year in the Appalachian community of Lucasville in southeastern Ohio, the Valley Local School District implemented a 30-minute bimonthly period at the Valley Middle School and tapped "student ambassadors" from the neighboring high school to focus on prescription drug abuse and other issues affecting students, from bullying to the proper use of social networking.

"It's about more than drugs," explains school counselor Jeff Rase. "It's building a positive culture in our school."

At the same time, Rase adds, prescription drugs are a primary topic, and with good reason in a poor community with a high unemployment rate. In a survey of Valley Middle School students before the program began, 42 percent identified prescription drugs as "very dangerous," compared to 75 percent and 56 percent when asked about marijuana and alcohol, respectively.

"Pills have become not only something to abuse and something addictive, but a driving force in our local economy. They're like money here," adds Roberts, also a nurse with the Portsmouth City Health Department in Scioto County, Ohio. "We've got little old grandmas and grandpas selling their pills (to drug abusers in the community) to supplement their Social Security income."

Through a $5,000 grant, Roberts is funding the ambassador program for eight districts in the county. The program trains high school students who are already leaders in student government and sports teams to work with their middle school peers about prescription drug abuse. "We're not going to be able to solve poverty," Roberts reasons. "But we can do some education in the schools so kids realize that prescription drug abuse isn't normal."

"It adds another relationship that they can look up to," says Rase, who plans to have middle school students become ambassadors to the district's elementary schools in the near future.

When it comes to any kind of drug abuse, Rase says, "we all know that peer influence is one of the biggest things we have to fight. So why not put a positive spin on peer relationships?"

Let's End the Prescription Drug Death Epidemic

Sanjay Gupta

Sanjay Gupta is associate chief of neurosurgery at Grady Memorial Hospital in Atlanta, Georgia, and CNN's chief medical correspondent.

It's the biggest man-made epidemic in the United States. That's how a doctor in Washington state described it to me as we sat outside the state capitol in Olympia.

He was talking about accidental death from prescription drug overdoses. The doctor, Gary Franklin, medical director for Washington state's Department of Labor and Industries, recounted terrifying case after case and told me it was the saddest thing he had ever seen.

I remember him telling me about a teenager dying because he had taken too much narcotic medication after a dental procedure.

The most common scenario, he said, involves a man in his 40s or 50s who visits a doctor with a backache and walks out with a pain pill prescription. About three years later, typically, the man dies in his sleep from taking too many pills, or mixing them with alcohol.

They Don't Intend to Die

They don't intend to die, but more than 20,000 times a year—every 19 minutes, on average—that is exactly what happens. Accidental overdoses are now a leading cause of accidental deaths in the United States, surpassing car crashes.

As a neurosurgeon working in a busy level 1 trauma hospital, I had an idea that the problem was growing—but the numbers still boggle the mind.

Distribution of morphine, the main ingredient in popular painkillers, increased 600% from 1997–2007, according to the U.S. Drug Enforcement Administration. In the United States, we now prescribe enough pain pills to give every man, woman and child one every four hours, around the clock, for three weeks.

We often pay close attention if a celebrity dies of an overdose, but truth is, it's our friends, neighbors and yes, our own family members who are dying.

In fact, the person who really brought the issue to my attention was former President Bill Clinton. He called me a few months ago, and I could immediately tell he was broken up about something. I had worked for him in the White House in the late '90s, talked to him countless times since then, and I had never heard him like this.

If you are awake you may not notice it, but if you fall asleep with too many of these pills in your system, you never wake up.

Two of his friends had both lost sons, he told me. The cause: accidental overdose.

I will never forget how he put it. "Look, no one thinks having a few beers and an Oxycontin is a good idea, but you also don't expect to die." I knew at that moment we needed to do our part in the media to shine a bright light on this issue and find solutions that work.

As a starting point, 80% of the world's pain pills are consumed right here in the United States, according to 2011 congressional testimony from the American Society of Interventional Pain Physicians.

No doubt, many are for perfectly legitimate reasons and are not misused or abused. Yet culturally, we have become increasingly intolerant of even minor amounts of pain and increasingly comfortable with taking heavy-duty medications.

The Perils of Pain Pills

We know, however, that after just a few months of taking the pills, something starts to change in the body. The effectiveness wears off, and patients typically report getting only about 30% pain relief, compared with when they started. Even more concerning, a subgroup of these patients develop a condition known as hyperalgesia, an increased sensitivity to pain.

As you might guess, all of this creates a situation where the person starts to take more and more pills. And even though they are no longer providing much pain relief, they can still diminish the body's drive to breathe.

If you are awake you may not notice it, but if you fall asleep with too many of these pills in your system, you never wake up. Add alcohol, and the problem is exponentially worse. People who take pain or sleeping pills and drink a couple glasses of wine are playing Russian roulette.

I am not at all sorry for coming off dramatic or scary as I write this. I only wish I had been this dramatic years ago.

Truth is, it is easier for a doctor to write a prescription than to explore other effective options to combat pain. And it is easier for patients to take those prescription pills than to search for alternatives themselves. Both those things must absolutely change. . . .

Clinton has dedicated a significant part of his post-presidency domestic efforts to this cause, and it will not come as a surprise that he has identified areas where we can all make a difference. . . .

Throughout my career, I have traveled the world and seen problems so intransigent that I thought solutions would never come. With accidental deaths due to prescription drugs, however, we have an opportunity to fix the problem and end this large man-made epidemic.

Fraud Involving Prescription Drug Abuse Is a Problem for Employers

Jay Krueger

Jay Krueger is chief strategy officer for PMSI, a provider of specialty workers compensation products and services.

Open the paper and you're likely to see an article on prescription drug abuse. On one hand, we're fortunate to live in a time when pain medications exist. On the other, the fact that these narcotics are so addictive presents society with a great challenge. As many workplace injuries involve chronic pain, the misuse of these drugs is a problem that threatens the health and lives of injured workers, prevents return-to-work and adds to workers comp [compensation] claims costs. But there are some steps companies can take to limit their exposure to this risk.

Ultimately, the challenge for the workers compensation industry is to facilitate the appropriate use of pain pills while preventing the misuse and waste of costly drugs. The goal is to help employees control their pain in a way that hastens their return to work and improves their quality of life. Preventing fraud and abuse helps everyone reach it.

In one actual workers comp claim case, an injured worker was prescribed four legitimate medications, a number not unusual for workers compensation cases. Because of these multiple prescriptions, however, the workers compensation pharmacy benefit management (PBM) firm identified him as a candidate for urine drug testing. The physician concurred, and a random urine test was ordered.

Jay Krueger, "Stemming Narcotics Fraud: Keeping Costs Down and Employees from Abusing Prescription Pills," *Risk Management Magazine*, vol. 59, no. 2, March 2012.

The testing found only two of the four prescription drugs present, while a fifth drug that had not been prescribed was detected. A review of the medication profile showed that the patient had been consistently filling the medications not present in the urine, thus suggesting compliance or diversion issues. Additionally, there were no prescriptions for the fifth drug.

Financial losses are only part of the negative implications of fraud and abuse. The clinical dangers are just as alarming.

Because of these inconsistent results, the injured worker was enrolled in a drug-testing and monitoring program. A few weeks later, however, further testing showed that the injured worker still was not complying with the prescribed therapy. Because there were narcotics present that should not have been there as well as the absence of prescribed narcotics, the prescriber chose to dismiss this individual from the clinical practice for violating the agreed-upon narcotic treatment plan. The PBM then informed the payer of the prescriber's decision to prevent the injured worker from finding an unsuspecting prescriber to continue the pattern of misuse.

A Prevalent Problem

This case is not unique. According to the latest annual drug trend report from workers comp service provider PMSI, 70% of total pharmacy spending in workers compensation is related to medications used to treat pain. And narcotic pain medications as a group accounted for 34% of overall drug costs. Claims involving schedule II opioids (such as Percocet and Oxycontin) incur an added cost of $20,000 per claim and a delay in return to work that is six times longer than the norm.

Financial losses are only part of the negative implication, of fraud and abuse. The clinical dangers are just as alarming. They include adverse drug reactions and drug therapy complications, cumulative side effects (such as sedation that impairs the patient's functional status and hampers the likelihood of return to work), and inappropriate dosing, which can lead to serious and sometimes fatal consequences.

How prevalent is the misuse and fraudulent use of narcotic drugs in workers compensation cases? PMSI detects the presence of two or more opioid prescribers (an indication of misuse) in almost 2.5% of the injured worker population suffering from chronic pain.

Another indication of the existence of misuse is the higher volumes of narcotic medications used in certain jurisdictions. Workers in Louisiana, Pennsylvania, Massachusetts and New York received significantly more narcotics per claim than in other states—up to 125% more—according to a report from the Workers Compensation Research Institute.

The study also found that only 7% of long-term narcotics users were screened for drugs, despite the fact that medical guidelines recommend periodic urine tests for drug screening for patients who are long-term users of narcotics. In the absence of this oversight, fraud is easier to perpetrate.

Clinical Pain Management

Clinical pain management programs deter narcotics fraud and abuse while helping to lower costs and improve patient outcomes. If you elect to use one, there are a four elements of a pain management program that risk managers should understand.

The first is a group of tools referred to as utilization control strategies. These are techniques that help manage access to drugs by weighing criteria to evaluate how appropriate and cost effective medication is. By scrutinizing the list of drugs that may be prescribed, ensuring that there is prior authorization for prescriptions, and converting patients to generic drugs when possible, there can be significant savings. Just by managing the list of drugs available to be prescribed, companies have seen an average savings of 28% in prescription drug costs per high-risk injured worker.

The second element is a targeted intervention program. Through this, administrators use analytics to cut down on the inappropriate use, duplication and potential abuse of medication. Methods include profiling high-risk patients and converting claimants from multiple prescribers to a single prescriber. Targeted intervention has shown a 90% success rate in eliminating multiple narcotic prescribers.

Next comes care management, which aims to improve medication-related outcomes for chronically injured, high-risk patients. One tool used is a medication review, in which a clinical pharmacist who specializes in pain management for occupational injuries assesses the patient's drug therapy and develops a plan for pain management. That may sound basic, but it often goes undone. Through this process alone, administrators have had a 64% success rate in eliminating inappropriate medication therapies.

Last—but perhaps most important—comes education. These programs can be vital for helping patients, prescribers and claims professionals understand the appropriate use of opioids. If all the parties involved become better versed in the true goals of pain control, it will greatly reduce the likelihood of opioid abuse and misappropriation.

The Federal Government Is Taking Action to Reduce Prescription Drug Abuse

Executive Office of the President of the United States

This is an official US government report prepared by the Office of the President.

Prescription drug abuse is the Nation's fastest-growing drug problem. While there has been a marked decrease in the use of some illegal drugs like cocaine, data from the National Survey on Drug Use and Health (NSDUH) show that nearly one-third of people aged 12 and over who used drugs for the first time in 2009 began by using a prescription drug non-medically. The same survey found that over 70 percent of people who abused prescription pain relievers got them from friends or relatives, while approximately 5 percent got them from a drug dealer or from the Internet. Additionally, the latest Monitoring the Future study—the Nation's largest survey of drug use among young people—showed that prescription drugs are the second most-abused category of drugs after marijuana. In our military, illicit drug use increased from 5 percent to 12 percent among active duty service members over a three-year period from 2005 to 2008, primarily attributed to prescription drug abuse.

Although a number of classes of prescription drugs are currently being abused, this action plan primarily focuses on the growing and often deadly problem of prescription opioid abuse. The number of prescriptions filled for opioid pain relievers—some of the most powerful medications available—has increased dramatically in recent years. From 1997 to 2007,

"Epidemic: Responding to America's Prescription Drug Abuse Crisis," Whitehouse.gov, 2011.

the milligram per person use of prescription opioids in the U.S. increased from 74 milligrams to 369 milligrams, an increase of 402 percent. In addition, in 2000, retail pharmacies dispensed 174 million prescriptions for opioids; by 2009, 257 million prescriptions were dispensed, an increase of 48 percent. Further, opiate overdoses, once almost always due to heroin use, are now increasingly due to abuse of prescription painkillers.

It is important to provide law enforcement agencies with support and the tools they need to expand their efforts to shut down "pill mills" and to stop "doctor shoppers."

These data offer a compelling description of the extent to which the prescription drug abuse problem in America has grown over the last decade, and should serve to highlight the critical role parents, patients, healthcare providers, and manufacturers play in preventing prescription drug abuse.

These realities demand action, but any policy response must be approached thoughtfully, while acknowledging budgetary constraints at the state and Federal levels. The potent medications science has developed have great potential for relieving suffering, as well as great potential for abuse. There are many examples: acute medical pain treatment and humane hospice care for cancer patients would be impossible without prescription opioids; benzodiazepines are the bridge for many people with serious anxiety disorders to begin the process of overcoming their fears; and stimulants have a range of valuable uses across medical fields. Accordingly, any policy in this area must strike a balance between our desire to minimize abuse of prescription drugs and the need to ensure access for their legitimate use. Further, expanding effective drug abuse treatment is critical to reducing prescription drug abuse, as only a small fraction of drug users are currently undergoing treatment.

This Prescription Drug Abuse Prevention Plan expands upon the Administration's *National Drug Control Strategy* and includes action in four major areas to reduce prescription drug abuse: education, monitoring, proper disposal, and enforcement. First, education is critical for the public and for healthcare providers to increase awareness about the dangers of prescription drug abuse, and about ways to appropriately dispense, store, and dispose of controlled substance medications. Second, enhancement and increased utilization of prescription drug monitoring programs will help to identify "doctor shoppers" and detect therapeutic duplication and drug-drug interactions. Third, the development of consumer-friendly and environmentally-responsible prescription drug disposal programs may help to limit the diversion of drugs, as most non-medical users appear to be getting the drugs from family and friends. Fourth, it is important to provide law enforcement agencies with support and the tools they need to expand their efforts to shut down "pill mills" and to stop "doctor shoppers" who contribute to prescription drug trafficking.

Educating prescribers on substance abuse is critically important, because even brief interventions by primary care providers have proven effective in reducing or eliminating substance abuse in people who abuse drugs but are not yet addicted to them.

Education

A crucial first step in tackling the problem of prescription drug abuse is to raise awareness through the education of parents, youth, patients, and healthcare providers. Although there have been great strides in raising awareness about the dangers of using illegal drugs, many people are still not aware that the misuse or abuse of prescription drugs can be as dangerous as the use of illegal drugs, leading to addiction and even death.

Parents and youth in particular need to be better educated about the dangers of the misuse and abuse of prescription drugs. There is a common misperception among many parents and youth that prescription drugs are less dangerous when abused than illegal drugs because they are [US Food and Drug Administration] FDA-approved. Many well-meaning parents do not understand the risks associated with giving prescribed medication to a teenager or another family member for whom the medication was not prescribed. Many parents are also not aware that youth are abusing prescription drugs; thus, they frequently leave unused prescription drugs in open medicine cabinets while making sure to lock their liquor cabinets. These misperceptions, coupled with increased direct-to-consumer advertising, which may also contribute to increased demand for medications, makes effective educational programs even more vital to combating prescription drug abuse.

In addition, prescribers and dispensers, including physicians, physicians assistants, nurse practitioners, pharmacists, nurses, prescribing psychologists, and dentists, all have a role to play in reducing prescription drug misuse and abuse. Most receive little training on the importance of appropriate prescribing and dispensing of opioids to prevent adverse effects, diversion, and addiction. Outside of specialty addiction treatment programs, most healthcare providers have received minimal training in how to recognize substance abuse in their patients. Most medical, dental, pharmacy, and other health professional schools do not provide in-depth training on substance abuse; often, substance abuse education is limited to classroom or clinical electives. Moreover, students in these schools may only receive limited training on treating pain. . . .

Educating prescribers on substance abuse is critically important, because even brief interventions by primary care providers have proven effective in reducing or eliminating substance abuse in people who abuse drugs but are not yet addicted to them. In addition, educating healthcare providers about prescription drug abuse will promote awareness of this growing problem among prescribers so they will not over-prescribe the medication necessary to treat minor conditions. This, in turn, will reduce the amount of unused medication sitting in medicine cabinets in homes across the country.

Planned Action

The following action items will be taken to improve educational efforts and to increase research and development:

Healthcare Provider Education:

- Work with Congress to amend Federal law to require practitioners (such as physicians, dentists, and others authorized to prescribe) who request DEA [Drug Enforcement Administration] registration to prescribe controlled substances to be trained on responsible opioid prescribing practices as a precondition of registration. This training would include assessing and addressing signs of abuse and/or dependence.

- Require drug manufacturers, through the Opioid Risk Evaluation and Mitigation Strategy (REMS), to develop effective educational materials and initiatives to train practitioners on the appropriate use of opioid pain relievers.

- Federal agencies that support their own healthcare systems will increase continuing education for their practitioners and other healthcare providers on proper prescribing and disposal of prescription drugs.

- Work with appropriate medical and healthcare boards to encourage them to require education curricula in health professional schools (medical, nursing, pharmacy, and dental) and continuing education programs to include instruction on the safe and appropriate use of opioids to treat pain while minimizing the risk of addiction and substance abuse. Additionally, work with relevant medical, nursing, dental, and pharmacy student groups to help disseminate educational materials, and establish student programs that can give community educational presentations on prescription drug abuse and substance abuse.

- In consultation with medical specialty organizations, develop methods of assessing the adequacy and effectiveness of pain treatment in patients and in patient populations, to better inform the appropriate use of opioid pain medications.

- Work with the American College of Emergency Physicians to develop evidence-based clinical guidelines that establish best practices for opioid prescribing in the Emergency Department.

- Work with all stakeholders to develop tools to facilitate appropriate opioid prescribing, including development of Patient-Provider Agreements and guidelines.

Parent, Youth, and Patient Education:

- Enlist all stakeholders to support and promote an evidence-based public education campaign on the appropriate use, secure storage, and disposal of prescription drugs, especially controlled substances. Engage local anti-drug coalitions, and other organizations (chain pharmacies, community pharmacies, boards of pharmacies, boards of medicine) to promote and disseminate public education materials and to increase awareness of prescription drug misuse and abuse.

- Require manufacturers, through the Opioid Risk Evaluation and Mitigation Strategy (REMS), to develop effective educational materials for patients on the appropriate use and disposal of opioid pain relievers.

- Working with private-sector groups, develop an evidence-based media campaign on prescription drug abuse, targeted to parents, in an effort to educate them about the risks associated with prescription drug abuse and the importance of secure storage and proper disposal of prescription drugs (including through public alerts or other approaches to capture the attention of busy parents).

Research and Development:

- Expedite research, through grants, partnerships with academic institutions, and priority New Drug Application review by FDA, on the development of treatments for pain with no abuse potential as well as on the development of abuse-deterrent formulations (ADF) of opioid medications and other drugs with abuse potential.

- Continue advancing the design and evaluation of epidemiological studies to address changing patterns of abuse.

- Provide guidance to the pharmaceutical industry on the development of abuse-deterrent drug formulations and on post-market assessment of their performance.

Tracking and Monitoring

Forty-three states have authorized prescription drug monitoring programs (PDMPs). PDMPs aim to detect and prevent the diversion and abuse of prescription drugs at the retail level, where no other automated information collection system exists, and to allow for the collection and analysis of prescription data more efficiently than states without such a program can accomplish. However, only thirty-five states have operational PDMPs. These programs are established by state legislation and are paid for by a combination of state and Federal funds. PDMPs track controlled substances prescribed by authorized practitioners and dispensed by pharmacies. PDMPs can and should serve a multitude of functions, including: assisting in patient care, providing early warning of drug abuse epidemics (especially when combined with other data), evaluating interventions, and investigating drug diversion and insurance fraud. . . .

The scale of the problem is vast with more than 7 million Americans reporting use of a prescription medication for non-medical purposes in the past 30 days.

PDMPs appear to be a promising approach, but more work is needed to determine how to maximize their effectiveness. Reducing prescription drug abuse requires a combination of Federal, state, and local action. All involved need to be informed on how to use available data sets to identify areas on which to concentrate their efforts. . . .

A major effort must be undertaken to improve the functioning of state PDMPs, especially regarding real-time data access by clinicians, and to increase inter-state operability and communication. Furthermore, we must identify stable financial support to maximize the utility of PDMPs, which will help reduce prescription drug diversion and provide better healthcare delivery. . . .

Proper Medication Disposal

Prescription drug abuse is a significant public health and public safety issue, and a large source of the problem is a direct result of what is in Americans' medicine cabinets. SAMHSA [Substance Abuse and Mental Health Services Administration]'s 2009 National Survey on Drug Use and Health found that over 70 percent of people who used prescription pain relievers non-medically got them from friends or relatives, while approximately 5 percent got them from a drug dealer or from the Internet. The same survey showed the scale of the problem is vast with more than 7 million Americans reporting use of a prescription medication for non-medical purposes in the past 30 days. Therefore, a comprehensive plan to address prescription drug abuse must include proper disposal of unused, unneeded, or expired medications. Providing individuals with a secure and convenient way to dispose of medications will help prevent diversion and abuse, and help to reduce the introduction of drugs into the environment.

A small group of practitioners ... abuse their prescribing privileges by prescribing these medications outside the usual course of professional practice or for illegitimate purposes.

In order to protect human health and the environment, it is vital that collected prescription drugs be appropriately disposed of in an environmentally safe manner. Thus, prescription drugs collected from individuals are to be disposed of in accordance with Federal, state, and local laws and regulations. Until prescription drug disposal programs are available to all communities, an important environmental safety message in the fight against improper medication disposal is to recommend against flushing prescription drugs with the few exceptions noted by the Food and Drug Administration (FDA). Instead of flushing, prescription drugs should be disposed of in sealed plastic bags with filler such as coffee grounds or kitty litter. However, due to public health concerns, the FDA does recommend disposal via flushing for certain opioid pain relievers that can pose life-threatening risks from accidental ingestion.

The following actions will be taken to increase proper disposal of prescription drugs and prevent diversion:

- While the administrative process to establish the DEA medication disposal rule is underway, DEA and other Federal agencies shall conduct additional take-back activities. Information about the take-back events shall be distributed to local anti-drug coalitions, HIDTA [High Intensity Drug Trafficking Areas], and other organizations (chain pharmacies, boards of pharmacies, boards of medicine, environmental agencies, etc).

- Once DEA regulations on controlled substance prescription drug disposal have been established, develop and execute a robust public education initiative to increase public awareness and provide education on new methods of safe and effective drug return and disposal.

- Once DEA regulations have been established, engage PhRMA [Pharmaceutical Research and Manufacturers of America] and others in the private sector to support community-based medication disposal programs.

Enforcement

Along with the increased legitimate use of prescription opioid medications in healthcare settings, there is also a small group of practitioners who abuse their prescribing privileges by prescribing these medications outside the usual course of professional practice or for illegitimate purposes. This has, in some areas, resulted in practitioners illegally prescribing and/or dispensing prescription controlled substances and other prescription drugs under the banner of medical care. These providers and clinics not only endanger the individuals receiving these medications, but also pose serious threats to the communities where they are located.

In addition, a number of "patient"-centered abuses have evolved, most notably "doctor shopping." Doctor shoppers visit multiple prescribers, in different locations within and outside of their states of residence, in order to receive controlled substances and other prescription drugs for diversion and/or abuse. These community-based problems require community-based solutions.

Prescription drug misuse and abuse is a major public health and public safety crisis.

The following actions will be taken to assist states to address doctor shopping and pill mills:

- ONDCP [Office of National Drug Control Policy], the National Methamphetamine and Pharmaceutical Initiative (NMPI), a law enforcement training initiative funded by HIDTA, and DEA will contribute to the curriculum for the pharmaceutical crime investigation and prosecution training program sponsored by BJA [Bureau of Justice Assistance] in 2011. Target training to states with the highest need.

- Increase training to law enforcement and prosecutor groups at national and regional conferences.

- Continue aggressive enforcement actions against pain clinics and prescribers who are not prescribing within the usual course of practice and not for legitimate medical purposes.

- Work with the appropriate groups to write and disseminate a Model Pain Clinic Regulation Law taking into consideration: 1) registration of these facilities with a state entity; 2) guidance for rules regarding number of employees, location, hours of operation; 3) penalties for operating, owning, or managing a non-registered pain clinic; 4) requirements for counterfeit-resistant prescription pads and reports of theft/loss of such pads; 5) disciplinary procedures to enforce the regulations; and 6) a procedure to allow patient records to be reviewed during regular state inspections.

- Increase HIDTA intelligence-gathering and investigation of prescription drug trafficking, and increase joint investigations by Federal, state, and local agencies.

- Identify and seek to remove administrative and regulatory barriers to "pill mill" and prescriber investigations that impair investigations while not serving another public policy goal.

- Expand the use of PDMP data to identify criminal prescribers and clinics by the volume of selected drugs prescribed. Encourage best practices for PDMPs, such as PDMP reporting of such prescribers and clinics to pharmacies, law enforcement, and insurance providers.

- Use PDMP data to identify "doctor shoppers" by their numbers of prescribers or pharmacies. Encourage best practices such as identifying such individuals to their prescribers and pharmacies, law enforcement and insurance providers.

Prescription Drug Abuse Plan Goals

National Drug Control Strategy Five Year Goal for Prescription Drug Abuse

- 15 percent reduction in non-medical use of prescription-type psychotherapeutic drugs in the past year among people 12 years of age and older. . . .

- Have legislation in all 50 states establishing Prescription Drug Monitoring Programs within 36 months;

- Expand by 10 percent, within 36 months, the available funding for treatment to increase access since only a small fraction of drug users currently undergo treatment;

- Decrease by 15 percent the number of unintentional overdose deaths related to opioids within 60 months.

Research and medicine have provided a vast array of medications to cure disease, ease suffering and pain, improve the quality of life, and save lives. This is no more evident than in the field of pain management. However, as with many new scientific discoveries and new uses for existing compounds, the potential for diversion, abuse, morbidity, and mortality are significant. Prescription drug misuse and abuse is a major public health and public safety crisis. As a Nation, we must take urgent action to ensure the appropriate balance between the benefits these medications offer in improving lives and the risks they pose. No one agency, system, or profession is solely responsible for this undertaking. We must address this issue as partners in public health and public safety. Therefore, ONDCP will convene a Federal Council on Prescription Drug Abuse, comprised of Federal agencies, to coordinate implementation of this prescription drug abuse prevention plan and will engage private parties as necessary to reach the goals established by the plan.

CHAPTER 4

What Other Problems Are Occurring with Prescription Drugs?

Chapter Preface

Famously, nineteenth-century physician and author Oliver Wendell Holmes wrote, "I firmly believe that if the whole materia medica [all medical drugs], as now used, could be sunk to the bottom of the sea, it would be all the better for mankind—and all the worse for the fishes." This statement is often quoted by people who believe that too many drugs are being prescribed to people who may be harmed by them, and in that context it is not merely exaggerated, but fundamentally controversial. However, the part about the fish—which was not meant literally at the time—is now known to be all too true. Damage to the environment from pharmaceuticals is already happening.

Residue from the drugs people take is excreted into the sewer system and in many cases cannot be filtered out by sewage treatment plants. Thus it ends up in rivers and ultimately in the sea, as does effluent, or liquid waste, from pharmaceutical factories. Recent laboratory studies have shown that these drugs alter the behavior of fish—for example, the anti-anxiety drug oxazepam makes perch bolder and less social, Prozac changes the way males interact with females, and the common over-the-counter drug ibuprofen reduces courtship behavior in zebrafish. What ecological effects such changes will have is not yet known, although sexual changes in wild fish have been observed and other forms of wildlife have occasionally been killed off. Considering the vast increase in human pharmaceutical consumption, environmental experts are worried.

The effect of pharmaceutical waste on the environment is only one of the problems raised by the increasing medical use of drugs. The more drugs adults have in their homes, the more children are accidentally poisoned by those not kept under lock and key. Moreover, babies who are born dependent on the drugs taken by their mothers during pregnancy suffer terribly from withdrawal symptoms. In short, even if prescription drugs were never abused, some harm apart from unpredictable side effects in patients would result from them. This is not to say that medication should be given up, any more than automobiles should be given up because of traffic accidents and air pollution. In both cases the benefits to people who are legitimately dependent on them are vital. But it does mean that as much care as possible must be taken to use drugs wisely and treat them with caution.

Not only are there problems connected with too many drugs, but there are some that result from too few—not counting the obvious problem of too many sick Americans being unable to afford them. Drugs to treat some of the illnesses most common in poor countries do not even exist, since unless drugs can be profitably sold, pharmaceutical companies cannot do the extensive research that would be required to develop them. And there are worldwide shortages of some drugs, especially those used in hospitals, that are badly needed—manufacturing cannot always keep up with the demand for them.

Even worse is the problem of counterfeit drugs. Criminals have found that they can make more money, and incur less risk, by selling fake prescription drugs than by dealing in illegal ones. This is not just a matter of selling them on the street to people who lack a legal source for them, although that certainly happens. Counterfeiters often sell their products to pharmaceutical suppliers, who unknowingly distribute them to reputable pharmacies. Thus even when a pill comes from a drugstore, it may not be real and thus may not have any effect on a patient's illness. It may even contain actively harmful ingredients.

This is not the only way that people can be harmed by legitimately-acquired drugs. Unfortunately, some doctors are induced to prescribe and even promote drugs about which they know too little by the tactics of pharmaceutical companies, which offer them free trips to conferences and pay prominent physicians to give speeches discussing new uses of drugs originally approved for specific purposes. Most of the doctors who are influenced assume that these uses are safe because they take the word of the speakers. But sometimes this assumption turns out to be wrong.

The goal of the government in requiring prescriptions for certain drugs is to protect the public from harm, but the system cannot prevent all instances of it. The US Food and Drug Administration (FDA) has considered changing more drugs from prescription to over-the-counter (OTC) status, which would enable more people to get those they need for minor, ongoing conditions without the expense and delay of visiting a doctor. But while the law requires all known side effects of prescription drugs to be stated in advertising and labeling, this is not true of OTC drugs. Even with respect to those now common, some people are harmed by effects of which they have not been warned. So such policy decisions are controversial, and it is difficult to strike the right balance between protection and the freedom of people to make their own decisions about their personal health.

Children Are Being Accidentally Poisoned by Adults' Prescription Drugs

Steven Reinberg

Steven Reinberg is a reporter for HealthDay.

As the number of adults taking prescription drugs has grown, so has the number of children being accidentally poisoned by them, a new study finds.

"We found between 2000 and 2009 [that] rates of pediatric exposure to adult medications were increasing," said lead researcher Dr. Lindsey Burghardt, from the division of emergency medicine at Boston Children's Hospital.

In addition, there was an association between the number of prescriptions written for these medications for adults and the increase in the number of children being poisoned by them, she said.

"This is the first step, to identify the extent of the problem," Burghardt said. "Despite all these precautions that have been put in place to try to prevent these poisonings in kids the problem persists," she said. "In fact, the number of poisonings has been increasing."

The next step is to try to identify why this is happening, Burghardt said. That, however, isn't clear at this point, she added.

Burghardt advises keeping these medications out of the reach of young children. Particularly, those under 5 who are at the greatest risk.

The greatest risk for teen misuse is from narcotic painkillers, Burghardt said, mostly intended for recreational use or to attempt suicide.

The report was published in the June 3 [2013] online edition of *Pediatrics*.

Kids Open Prescription Bottles

"What we see a lot is open prescription bottles from parents or grandparents, and ingestion of diabetic and other drugs by kids," said Dr. Vincenzo Maniaci, a pediatric emergency medicine doctor at Miami Children's Hospital. "Kids are going to get into everything."

Medications need to be kept high up, in locked boxes, so children can't get at them, Maniaci said. Medications should not be kept on countertops, in purses or on nightstands.

If a parent suspects a child had ingested a prescription medication, the first step is to call poison control, Maniaci said.

The most serious injuries and hospitalizations ... were caused by narcotic painkillers and diabetes drugs.

To try to get a handle on the extent of the problem, Burghardt's team used the National Poison Data System surveys for 2000 through 2009 to track poisoning from prescription drugs among infants to 5-year-olds, children aged 6 to 12 and teens aged 13 to 19.

Specifically, they looked at poisoning from drugs used to treat diabetes, high cholesterol and high blood pressure, as well as narcotic painkillers.

They found young children had the greatest risk of being poisoned by diabetes drugs (60.2 percent) and blood pressure drugs (59.7 percent).

The most serious injuries and hospitalizations, however, were caused by narcotic painkillers and diabetes drugs.

Prescription pills aren't the only drugs kids are finding and taking. A recent study in the online edition of *JAMA Pediatrics* found that since medical marijuana was legalized in Colorado, more than a dozen young children have been unintentionally poisoned with the drug.

About half of the cases resulted from kids eating marijuana-laced cookies, brownies, sodas or candy. In many cases, the marijuana came from their grandparents' stash, the investigators said.

But doctors aren't familiar with marijuana poisoning in children, so unless the parents are forthcoming it can take time and tests to diagnose the problem, the Colorado researchers explained. Symptoms of marijuana poisoning in children include sleepiness and balance problems while walking.

Babies Are Being Born Addicted to Prescription Drugs

Associated Press

The Associated Press is an American news agency that produces articles that appear in news outlets throughout the world.

He's less than two weeks old, but he has the telltale signs of a baby in pain: a sore on his chin where he's rubbed the skin raw, along with a scratch on his cheek. He suffers from so many tremors that nurses watch him around the clock in case he starts seizing—or stops breathing.

The baby is one of many infants born dependent on drugs. He is being treated at East Tennessee Children's Hospital in Knoxville, where doctors and nurses are on the front lines fighting the nation's prescription drug epidemic. Drug abuse in the state [of Tennessee] is ranked among the nation's highest, according to some estimates.

The hospital expects to treat 320 children this year [2013] for drug dependence, known as neonatal abstinence syndrome—up from 33 in 2008. Last year, the hospital treated 283.

"It blew us away," Andrew Pressnell, a nurse at the unit, said of the dramatic increase. "We didn't know what to do."

States across the US have passed laws to crack down on prescription drug abuse, including in the poor, mountainous Appalachian region, where the drugs were easily available as they flowed north from so-called "pill mills" in Florida.

The US government doesn't track the number of babies born dependent on drugs. A study published last year in the

Journal of the American Medical Association found that more than 13,000 infants were affected across the US in 2009.

Tennessee is the first state to track the number of babies born dependent on prescription drugs, said Stephen W. Patrick, a neonatologist at the University of Michigan and one of the authors of the study.

Babies in Pain

The preferred way to treat drug-dependent babies at the Tennessee hospital is by giving them small doses of an opiate and gradually weaning them off, said Dr. John Buchheit, who heads the neonatology unit. So every few hours, the staff will give the infants morphine to help them get their symptoms of withdrawal under control. They'll be weaned off over a period of either days or weeks, Buchheit said.

"The problem is the side effects of morphine," Buchheit said. "The one we worry about—the biggie—is that it can cause you to stop breathing."

A small army of volunteers called "cuddlers" help the [hospital] staff by holding the [drug-dependent] infants, rocking them and helping them ride out their symptoms.

Roughly half of the neonatal unit's 49 infants are being treated for drug dependence. For those infants, the pain can be excruciating. The doctors and nurses who treat them say the babies can suffer from nausea, vomiting, severe stomach cramps and diarrhea.

"Diarrhea so bad that their bottoms will turn red like somebody has dipped them in scalding water and blistered and bled," said Carla Saunders, a neonatal nurse practitioner who helps coordinate the treatment at the hospital.

They have trouble eating, sleeping and in the worst cases suffer from seizures. Many suffer from skin conditions and tremors. Nurses place mittens on their hands because the babies get so agitated that they constantly scratch and rub their faces.

And they are inconsolable.

A small army of volunteers called "cuddlers" help the staff by holding the infants, rocking them and helping them ride out their symptoms.

Many of the babies have private, dark rooms with high-tech rocking machines to keep them calm.

Bob Woodruff, one of the 57 cuddlers for the hospital, gently rocks Liam, a 10-day-old infant who was born drug-dependent. The 71-year-old retired professor moves from room to room, wherever he's needed.

"It's very satisfying," he said.

It is impossible to be unmoved by these infants, said Saunders, the neonatal nurse practitioner.

"If there is anything that could drive the people in our society to stop turning their heads to adult addiction," she said, "it's going to be the babies."

Part of the solution to drug-addicted babies is better education—Tennessee Department of Health Commissioner John Dreyzehner is part of a group lobbying the Food and Drug Administration to put a warning on prescription drug bottles of the dangers of taking drugs while pregnant.

Prescription Drug Residue Harms Wildlife and the Environment

Sonia Shah

Sonia Shah is an author and science journalist whose writing has appeared in many national publications. She is the author of three books.

The standard that new drugs be safe for human consumption was first enshrined in U.S. regulations in 1938, after an antibacterial drug dissolved in a poisonous solvent killed 100 children. Now, armed with a range of evidence suggesting that wildlife and human health may be threatened by pharmaceutical residues that escape into waterways and elsewhere, a growing band of concerned ecotoxicologists and environmental chemists are calling for yet another standard for new medications: that they be designed to be safe for the environment.

The movement for "green pharmacy," as it has been dubbed, has grown as new technology has allowed scientists to discern the presence of chemicals in the environment at minute concentrations, revealing the wide dispersal of human and veterinary drugs across the planet. In recent years, scientists have detected trace amounts of more than 150 different human and veterinary medicines in environments as far afield as the Arctic. Eighty percent of the U.S.'s streams and nearly a quarter of the nation's groundwater sampled by the United States Geological Survey (USGS) has been found to be contaminated with a variety of medications.

This contamination is poised to worsen as the global appetite for medications swells. The drug industry sold $773 billion worth of drugs worldwide in 2008, more than double the amount sold in 2000, and with an aging population and ever-cheaper manufacturing, pharmaceutical production is expected to grow 4 to 7 percent annually until at least 2013. Americans bring home more than 10 prescription drugs per capita per year, consuming an estimated 17 grams of antibiotics alone—more than three times the per capita rate of consumption in European countries such as Germany. U.S. live-stock consume even more, with farmers dispensing 11,000 metric tons of antimicrobial medications every year, mainly to promote the growth of animals.

Poisoned Vultures

Drugging our bodies inevitably drugs our environment, too, as many medications can pass through our bodies and waste treatment facilities virtually intact. And it is difficult to predict where and how unexpectedly vulnerable creatures may accrue potentially toxic doses. Take, for example, the ongoing mass poisoning of vultures in South Asia by anti-arthritis painkillers.

Scientists have discovered a range of adverse effects in wildlife exposed to pharmaceutical residues.

The popular anti-inflammatory and arthritis drug, di-clofenac, is sold worldwide under more than three dozen different brand names, and is used in both human and veterinary medicine. In India, farmers started dosing their cows and oxen with the drug in the early 1990s to relieve inflammation that could impair the animals' ability to provide milk or pull plows. Soon, about 10 percent of India's livestock harbored some 300 micrograms of diclofenac in their livers. When they died, their carcasses were sent to special dumps and picked clean by flocks of vultures. It was an efficient system, for un-like feral dogs and plague-infested rats, South Asia's abundant vulture population—estimated at more than 60 million in the early 1990s—carried no human pathogens and was resistant to livestock diseases such as anthrax.

But vultures who fed on the treated carcasses accrued a dose of diclofenac of around 100 micrograms per kilogram. A person with arthritis would need 10 times that amount to feel an effect, but it was enough to devastate the vultures. Between 2000 and 2007, the South Asian vulture population declined by 40 percent every year; today, 95 percent of India's Gyps vultures and 90 percent of Pakistan's are dead, due primarily to the diclofenac that scientists have found lurking in their tissues. South Asian and British scientists who experimentally exposed captive vultures to diclofenac-dosed buffalo found that the birds went into renal failure—scientists still don't know why—and died within days of exposure. As the vulture population has declined, the feral dog population has boomed, and the Indian government's attempt to control the rabies they carry has started to flounder.

The governments of India, Pakistan, and Nepal banned veterinary use of diclofenac in 2006, but the drug has still not disappeared from livestock tissues. And last year scientists found that another arthritis drug—ketoprofen—is similarly deadly for the birds.

Background levels of antibiotics in the environment may be hastening the emergence of difficult-to-control antibiotic-resistant pathogens.

Contaminated Water

The poisoning of vultures, while dramatic, is not the only worrisome impact of our medicated environment. Scientists have discovered a range of adverse effects in wildlife exposed to pharmaceutical residues, from impaired reproduction to less-fit offspring.

For example, freshwater habitats around the world have been found contaminated with the synthetic estrogen used in contraceptive pills, ethynylestradiol. While concentrations are generally found around .5 nanograms per liter, concentrations as high as several hundred nanograms per liter have been reported, as well. A large body of evidence has connected this contamination with excess feminization in fish. In one study, U.S. and Canadian government scientists purposely contaminated an experimental lake in Ontario with around 5 nanograms per liter of ethynyl estradiol, and studied the effects on the lake's fathead minnow population, a common species that fish like lake trout and northern pike feed on. Minnows normally become sexually mature at two years of age and enjoy a single mating season before perishing. Exposed to ethynyl estradiol, the male minnows' testicular development was arrested and they started making early-stage eggs instead. That year's mating season was disastrous. Within two years, the minnow population crashed.

Recent findings in New England of higher concentrations of hermaphroditic frogs around suburban and urban waterways, compared to those in undisturbed and agricultural areas, have led to suspicions that synthetic estrogens may be exerting a similarly disruptive effect on amphibians, according to Yale University ecologist David Skelly, who is currently investigating the possibility.

Resistant Bacteria

Our drugged environment could also affect human health. Background levels of antibiotics in the environment may be hastening the emergence of difficult-to-control antibiotic-resistant pathogens. Bacteria share genes across species, and so any increased drug resistance in one species can cross into other, more pathogenic species. As one might suspect, scientists have found that drug-resistant bacteria populations are much more common in environments where antibiotics are heavily used. For example, in samples from dairy farms where livestock are treated, and from lakes that receive effluent from hospitals, antibiotic-resistant bacteria are up to 70 percent more common than in uncontaminated environments. The facilities that must manage such antibiotic waste, by using the metabolic capacity of bacteria to treat the wastewater, become "selection machines for resistant bacteria," says University of Gothenburg [in Sweden] physiology professor Joakim Larsson.

Experimental evidence suggests that the witch's brew of drugs, pesticides, and other trace chemicals in the environment could be acting synergistically to ratchet up the adverse effects on wildlife. Scientists have tried to reproduce the effects of these mixtures by studying the impacts of combinations of compounds commonly found together in the environment—analyzing, for example, the effects of trace amounts of the antidepressant, fluoxetine, and the herbicide clofibric acid. They've found that low concentrations of fluoxetine have no effect on water fleas. Nor do low concentrations of clofibric acid. But if water fleas are exposed to both compounds in combination, the mixture will kill more than half.

Similarly, water fleas suffer no adverse effect when exposed to low concentrations of the antibiotics erythromycin, triclosan, and trimethoprim. But if exposed to all three simultaneously, scientists have found, water fleas' sex ratios become skewed.

Such impacts may intensify as the climate changes, especially in poor, arid countries. Countries with few resources and little water are more likely to recycle wastewater into drinking water, particularly as their regions become more arid, increasing the concentrations of pharmaceuticals and other contaminants. "This is becoming a more potent problem," says University of Freiburg [in Germany] environmental chemist and leading green-pharmacy advocate Klaus Kümmerer. "We may have a closed cycle, and compounds may become enriched."

Unpredictable Effects

Environmental toxicologists agree that while many of the adverse effects they've found in wildlife have been subtle, there is nothing preventing a vulture-like die-off from pharma poisoning elsewhere. "The vultures would have been a tough one to predict," says Mitchell Kostich, who studies the ecological risks of pharmaceuticals at the U.S. Environmental Protection Agency (EPA). "Are we going to be able to predict those kind of cases?"

Drug-makers should . . . consider environmental impact before *new drugs are brought to market.*

Given the current state of knowledge and today's regulatory infrastructure, probably not. Diclofenac was first launched in the mid-1970s, before regulators in the U.S. or Europe required environmental assessments of new drugs. Today, the U.S. Food and Drug Administration (FDA) only requires drug companies to file an environmental assessment if drugmakers plan to manufacture more than 40 tons of a drug. In 2008, just 20 out of more than 10,000 claimants were required to file such an assessment. And the FDA only requires assessments of a single manufacturer's contribution, not the total volume of the drug that may be produced or leaked into the environment.

Even if a comprehensive environmental assessment had been required, it is unlikely that diclofenac's effect on vultures would have been detected. Toxicity testing on wildlife is generally conducted on aquatic species, under the assumption that most environmental exposures to pharmaceuticals will occur via wastewater. The most commonly used species for such testing is the crustacean *Daphnia*, also known as the water flea. "If there is an effect on *Daphnia*, there may be an effect on other organisms," says Kümmerer, "But there is no organism that is the most sensitive organism. Test organisms are a compromise between sensitivity and ease of rearing in the lab, and availability."

And some species, such as Old World vultures, have idiosyncratic reactions. "Chickens could eat diclofenac and have no effect," notes Brunel University [in London, United Kingdom] ecotoxicologist John Sumpter. So could New World vultures, who likewise seem mysteriously impervious to the drug. And neither FDA nor European Union rules empower regulators to ban a human medicine based solely on environmental concerns.

A New Approach

While EPA and USGS scientists hope to figure out which pharmaceuticals are most dangerous in the environment and help wastewater treatment facilities learn how to screen for and treat them, green-pharmacy advocates such as Kümmerer are calling for a whole new approach to medicine-making. They argue that rather than aim for the most biologically potent, long-lasting compounds—the miracle cures that have long been the Holy Grail of pharmacology—drug-makers should create drugs that are "benign by design" and should consider environmental impact *before* new drugs are brought to market. Such an approach could lead to a new category of "green drugs": compounds that biodegrade quickly and easily in the environments they inevitably end up in.

Drug companies have already made strides in reducing waste in manufacturing because it saves them money and energy, Kümmerer says. But in order to convince companies to consider a drug's environmental impact, extra incentives will most likely be required. One incentive put forward by the European Environment Agency in January [2010] would involve extending patent protection for drugs that are safe, effective, and environmentally friendly.

That alone, by providing a solid boost to profit margins, could prove a powerful incentive for drug companies, and could help unleash a new generation of more easily degradable green drugs. Such drugs will not be as easy to store and distribute as today's drugs, though. Sensitive to sunlight and heat, they'll be more likely to be packaged in darkened bottles and require refrigeration. And then it will be up to us, as patients, to choose them anyway—and heal ourselves without sickening our environment.

Counterfeit Prescription Drugs Are Often Sold and Can Be Deadly

Richard Console

Richard Console is the founding and managing partner of Console and Hollawell, a personal injury law firm in New Jersey.

"Take two and call me in the morning," your doctor tells you. But sometimes two pills, or ten pills, or a hundred pills, will never have the intended effect. That's because these pills—often legally prescribed by a physician and legally purchased from a pharmacy—are in fact counterfeit medications. They can't cure a cough or treat malaria, and they certainly can't kill cancer cells. They pose an international problem so serious that an estimated 100,000 people die each year because of them, according to CNN.

If you're not outraged, maybe you should be.

These 100,000 people are someone's children, someone's parents, someone's spouses, someone's siblings or cousins or best friends. It happens in China, Africa, India—and, yes, it happens in the United States. Counterfeit drugs could be inside your medicine cabinet even as you read this sentence.

We talk about the placebo effect, the positive impact of believing that we are receiving medications that will help us. The placebo effect has been documented to help patients with a variety of conditions, often when the fake medication is being used in the role of a painkiller.

You could argue that any method that works to decrease a patient's pain without the risks outweighing the benefits is a good thing. But counterfeit pills, injections, or procedures have no direct impact on the condition itself. That means that diseases aren't getting better. When those conditions are as serious as malaria, blood clots, and cancer, giving patients fake drugs is as good as not treating them at all.

Creating counterfeit prescription drugs may be viewed as the latest get-rich-quick scheme, with less cost and risk than the illegal drug trade.

Counterfeit medications make up an estimated 10 percent of all drugs on the market throughout the world, the *Washington Post* reported [in 2012]. Though the prevalence of fake medications is estimated to be significantly lower in the United States—between 1 and 2 percent of medications, according to the National Association of Boards of Pharmacy—counterfeit versions of even a fraction of all prescription drugs sold in America can be deadly. "With more than 4 billion prescriptions filled in the United States each year—worth an estimated $310 billion—even 1 percent translates to 4 million packages," said TurnTo23.com, powered by ABC News.

That number could be growing. "With more medicines and drug ingredients for sale in the U.S. being manufactured overseas, American authorities are afraid more counterfeits will find their way into this country, putting patients' lives at risk," reported *USA Today*.

Why Do Counterfeit Drugs Exist?

That astronomical $310 billion figure plays a big part to explain why the illegal counterfeit drug industry exists at all. "Counterfeiters can make several million dollars quickly and, if they're caught, get off with as little as six months in jail," reported *USA Today*. With relatively low operating costs and the prospect of a high return on investment, creating counterfeit prescription drugs may be viewed as the latest get-rich-quick scheme, with less cost and risk than the illegal drug trade. "They are out to make money and simply do not care who gets hurt, or even dies, in the process," said CNN of counterfeit drug creators.

Some counterfeit drugs are simply ineffective, with no or minimal levels of active ingredients. . . . Others contain toxic ingredients.

While some of these dangerous counterfeit drugs are bought illegally by individual consumers seeking a way to afford the medications they need—which is hard to do with the skyrocketing price of such drugs, especially for uninsured patients—the fake medications problem isn't limited to these buyers. Unfortunately, you can't assume that your pills are safe just because you bought them from the pharmacy down the street. So many medications and medication ingredients are imported from suppliers outside the United States (and far beyond any direct governmental supervision) that you could be doing everything right, and still find yourself with the wrong medication.

Though any number of prescription medications could theoretically be counterfeited and sold, recent cases in the United States have made headlines:

- Blood-thinners: Counterfeit versions of the blood-thinning injection heparin contributed to the deaths of 149 Americans between 2007 and 2008, according to the *New York Times*. Blood thinners are most often used in patients who have suffered a blood clot or pulmonary embolism.

- Cancer medications: At least 19 physicians and clinics received the fake versions of the cancer medication Avastin, which did not contain the active ingredient necessary to treat cancer, according to *USA Today*.

Other prescription drugs that have been the focus of counterfeit medication horror stories across the globe include those for central nervous system disorders, heart conditions, high cholesterol, hypertension, erectile dysfunction, AIDS, psychiatric disorders, tuberculosis, and even teething syrup for babies. Some counterfeit drugs are simply ineffective, with no or minimal levels of active ingredients, according to the National Crime Prevention Council. Others contain toxic ingredients. All have the potential to seriously endanger the already fragile health of an ill or injured patient.

Toxic Ingredients

SafeMedicine.org reports that the following hazardous and even disgusting ingredients have been found in counterfeit or contaminated drugs:

- Arsenic

- Cadmium

- Chrome

- Lead

- Mercury

- Brick dust

- Chalk

- Drywall and sheet rock

- Floor wax

- Paint and paint thinner

- Antifreeze

- Rat poison

- Boric acid

- PCBs

- Benzopyrenes

Okay, these fillers sound pretty disgusting, but are they actually dangerous? As it turns out, yes. You're probably heard of arsenic as a poison, and you may be familiar with the toxic properties of lead and mercury, but all of these heavy metals (including cadmium and chrome) can have detrimental impacts on your skin, bones, teeth, liver, kidneys, and central nervous system—in other words, some of the most important parts of your body.

Everyday items seem harmless enough if you're not ingesting them, but when they end up inside your medication, they can be dangerous. Ingesting enough brick dust, chalk, drywall, floor wax, paint, or paint thinner can lead to difficulty breathing, blurred vision, vomiting, and even comas, potentially ending in death. Consuming rat poison and boric acid may result in kidney damage or even kidney failure. Benzopyrenes are known carcinogens. PCBS, or polychlorinated biphenyls, can cause certain types of cancer in women as well as developmental disorders.

The Drugs Must Stop Here

It's tragic enough when we hear of crises like counterfeit drugs killing and injuring our global neighbors, but when the problem occurs right here in our own pharmacies and doctor's offices, the frightening scenario becomes undeniably personal. Our families face this risk every single time they take a prescription medication. These drugs intended to heal could do real harm—often by doing nothing at all.

Though concerns about counterfeit drugs have been around for years, the issue made news headlines in 2012 due to an FDA [US Food and Drug Administration] warning and again in early 2013, when experts from the Institute of Medicine advised regulators to impose stricter policies to prevent counterfeit drugs from entering the United States market. Even now, though, little enough is heard about this predicament.

For the individuals whose lives are impacted by the danger—like parents of children diagnosed with curable cancer or husbands and wives whose spouses have been stricken by heart disease—counterfeit drugs have not been in the news enough. Awareness of the problem is still lacking.

It's this simple: No one should have to be sickened by toxic filler materials. No one should lose a family member because the medicine used to treat a curable disease had no medical ingredients in it at all.

Increasing Shortages of Prescription Drugs Put Patients at Risk

Jill Wechsler

Jill Wechsler is a Washington, DC-based reporter specializing in federal and state health-care issues.

The outcry from physicians, pharmacists, and patients over disruptions in supplies of vital medications continues to draw attention on Capitol Hill and throughout the healthcare system. Oncologists can't obtain widely-used chemotherapies to treat seriously ill patients. Doctors struggle to provide vital parenteral products for premature babies. Pharmacists have to search for alternate sources of important medications and home-infusion products. Surgeons are postponing operations because key anesthetics and pain medications are not available.

While there always have been periodic drug shortages, the problem has become much more acute in the last 2 years. The University of Utah Drug Information Service recorded more than 260 prescription drug shortages in 2011, topping 211 in 2010 and much more than in previous years when totals usually were well below 100. The vast majority involves sterile injectables, including many widely used generic analgesics, antibiotics, and chemotherapies. A survey by the American Hospital Association last June [2011] found that virtually all hospitals experienced at least 1 drug shortage last year, and multiple supply problems were common.

More recently, reports have surfaced of patients desperately asking pharmacists for medications to treat attention-deficit hyperactivity disorder (ADHD), 1 of the more severe shortage situations affecting retail pharmacies. Manufacturers blame government policies that limit production of controlled drug substances to prevent illegal diversion, while the regulators point to brand drug companies curbing production of low-cost generics to build sales of more expensive therapies. Patients forced to try alternative ADHD therapies ran the risk of adverse reactions and reimbursement problems.

Some companies voluntarily inform FDA of problems likely to lead to short supplies, but most do not, or act too late.

Multiple Factors

As the drug shortage crisis has made headlines, Congress has expanded investigations into the causes and responses to pharma supply chain difficulties. Some observers charge that too-strict oversight of manufacturing processes by FDA [US Food and Drug Administration] aggravates the problem—while others blame manufacturer negligence and business practices that lead to production errors that put the public health at risk. Some point a finger at government policies that drive down reimbursement for old-line generics, which discourages pharmaceutical industry investment in low-profit therapeutic categories that are difficult to produce.

In fact, a long list of underlying factors appears responsible for the manufacturing failures that have generated many short-supply situations. These include drug industry consolidation, limited raw material supplies, changes in inventory and distribution practices, production delays, increases in demand, and business decisions to close a manufacturing site or discontinue production. When there are only 1 or 2 sources for a critical drug, a small shift in production lines, plus just-in-time inventory controls at hospitals, make it hard to buffer the impact, explained pharmacist Richard Paoletti of Lancaster (Pa.) General Health at a September 2011 hearing on Capitol Hill.

An FDA public workshop that same month provided a forum for physicians, pharmacists, patient advocates, drug distributors, and manufacturers to air concerns and propose remedies for short-supply situations. Several Congressional committees held hearings last fall on the growing crisis. The outcry prompted the [Barack] Obama administration to unveil a drug shortages initiative in October 2011, and to issue an executive order for FDA and the Department of Justice to crack down on stockpiling and exorbitant pricing of low-supply drugs. The White House voiced support for legislation that expands advance reporting by manufacturers to FDA regarding production issues likely to lead to shortages.

A main problem is that FDA often does not know about looming drug supply problems because, under current law, only sole-source manufacturers of critical medications have to notify the agency when they anticipate product discontinuation. Some companies voluntarily inform FDA of problems likely to lead to short supplies, but most do not, or act too late.

Legislative Efforts to Ease Shortages

In early 2011, two senators introduced the Preserving Access to Life Saving Medications Act, which would require manufacturers to notify FDA when they discontinue a product or experience a production interruption. This proposed legislation would require 6 months' advance notification to FDA of production changes for a broad range of prescription drugs. And recently, representatives introduced legislation that expands the early warning system to include the cause, duration, and severity of shortages. The House version of the bill would impose penalties on manufacturers that fail to comply, along with leeway for companies that show they could not anticipate a manufacturing problem. Sudden production problems can occur without warning due to equipment breakdowns, plant fires, earthquakes, volcanoes, and other natural disasters.

FDA was able to prevent 195 drug shortages in 2011 through early notification and collaboration with manufacturers to avert problems, reported Sandra Kweder, an official in FDA's Center for Drug Evaluation and Research (CDER), at a hearing before the Senate Health, Education, Labor, and Pensions (HELP) Committee in December. When FDA knows of a possible supply interruption, its staff can move to prevent it by expediting approval of new suppliers, alternative production sites, and/or changes in product specifications. FDA reports some success in encouraging other firms to ramp up production or to enter a depleted market. The agency also can bend the rules to fill a supply gap by permitting continued marketing of a violative, but not dangerous, product or allowing temporary importation of a therapy approved overseas but not in the United States. . . .

FDA also wants manufacturers to be more flexible in disclosing information that they usually consider confidential, such as the reasons behind particular shortages and the likely duration. The aim is to help providers and patients understand the need to switch to alternate therapies or take other steps to maintain good health.

Revising Practices and Prices

So far, most pharmacists have been skeptical that regulatory actions will do much to alleviate problems in obtaining short-supply medications. In a recent survey of *Drug Topics'* readers, almost half (48%) of nearly 1,300 respondents predicted that the White House executive order will do little to help the situation; another 35% said that the administration's action is helpful, but that much more needs to be done.

An analysis by Congress' Government Accountability Office issued in December calls for FDA to beef up its fairly small drug shortages staff, establish a better information system to track data on shortages, and develop performance metrics to assess how well it's doing. Some providers want FDA to adjust how it calculates risks and benefits from regulatory actions to give greater weight to patient safety issues that arise from shortages.

Providers and patients also seek action to prevent hoarding and price gouging related to drug shortages.

FDA officials agree with these proposals and outlined in an October 2011 report how it is moving forward to implement needed change. Staffers are meeting with manufacturers to further discuss notification requirements. The agency is increasing its drug shortages staff and working to improve its drug-supply database. FDA also acknowledges the need to be sensitive to the impact on drug supplies of enforcement actions, such as instituting a drug recall or seizure. Agency officials maintain that they don't shut down a pharmaceutical plant for minor violations, but only take action when inspectors find significant problems with drug sterility and contamination, such as glass and metal particles in vials.

Providers and patients also seek action to prevent hoarding and price gouging related to drug shortages. FDA and the Justice Department are looking closely at the flood of faxes and phone calls from gray market profiteers to pharmacists and health professionals offering scarce drugs at huge markups.

In addition, legitimate, but steep, increases in acquisition costs of short-supply drugs create serious economic problems for retail pharmacies because both public and private payers delay adjustments to reimbursement for months. The National Community Pharmacists Association seeks legislation to raise generic dispensing rates for drugs experiencing shortages and to require more frequent updates to reimbursement standards for critical drugs covered by Medicare Part D plans.

Prevention Is Key

The ultimate goal for all stakeholders is to prevent shortages from occurring in the first place. One encouraging piece of news, says Joseph Hill, director of federal legislative affairs for the American Society for Health-System Pharmacists, is that a number of generic drug manufacturers are making significant investments in new plants and are bringing new production technologies online. Expanded production could be encouraged further by new user fees to support the regulation of generic drugs, which Congress is slated to approve this year [2012] to help bring new generics to market more quickly. An option under discussion is to offer relief from application fees for manufacturers seeking approval for new short-supply products.

Another proposal is that the federal government establish stockpiles for medically necessary drugs, as is done for treatments to protect against bioterrorist attacks and pandemics. And some consumer advocates urge antitrust officials to scrutinize proposed pharma company mergers with an eye on how the combination would affect limited drug supplies.

FDA is looking at strategies for developing a sentinel reporting network that would provide early signals of potential supply problems. This would involve identifying reporting sites among healthcare systems, wholesalers, and providers able to produce timely reports on shortage situations.

FDA's drug shortages staff also seeks to develop models for assessing the probability of future shortages, based on supply data, manufacturer characteristics, and market factors. Such a project would require analysis of data on thousands of marketed drugs and extensive model development and validation; a key challenge would be identifying a control group of drugs not in shortage. Whether such a project is feasible is not clear, FDA officials acknowledge. But they are considering it, the agency states, because "of the inherent public health value of preventing shortages before they occur."

"We will always have a certain amount of drug shortages out there," Hill concedes. The goal, he says, "is to bring it down to a level that is more manageable." He advises pharmacists to constantly monitor drug shortage websites for information on supplies and on therapeutic alternatives. Retail pharmacies increasingly call competitors and back-up wholesalers about needed supplies, and routinely start back-ordering a drug as soon as they learn of a supply problem. And they will push for legislation that expands FDA's ability to obtain more advance information from manufacturers and that addresses hoarding and pricing issues. These and other actions may help alleviate the current drug supply crisis.

Prescription Drug Shortages Impact Community Pharmacies

Drug shortages are also affecting community pharmacists and the patients they serve, according to a recent survey by the National Community Pharmacists Association (NCPA).

The NCPA survey of 675 community pharmacists found that drug shortages have resulted in an inability to fill prescriptions, higher acquisition costs, and lack of health insurance coverage for alternative medications, according to an NCPA statement.

In the past 6 months, 96% of the pharmacists who responded to the survey had experienced a drug shortage, and 59% had felt the impact daily and 23% weekly. Drug shortages are definitely delaying patient care, with the average drug shortage lasting 3 weeks or longer. Patients were unable to obtain their needed supply from alternative pharmacies, according to 78% of the survey respondents.

Doctors Receive Incentives for Promoting Untested Uses of Existing Drugs

Kathleen Sharp

Kathleen Sharp is an award-winning investigative journalist and author of Blood Medicine: Blowing the Whistle on One of the Deadliest Prescription Drugs Ever *as well as several other books.*

As the crimson sun slipped into the gray Pacific Ocean, a multibillion-dollar drug deal took shape. A group of board-certified doctors greeted each other in a private room at a luxury hotel in California. The oncologists were big buyers of an anti-anemia drug called Procrit, sold by Ortho Biotech, a Johnson & Johnson (J&J) division. That Friday evening, the company toasted its top clients and their wives with bottles of Beaujolais, porterhouse steaks and free weekend accommodations.

The event could have been just another "grin and grip" affair, but there was a catch: J&J wanted to pump the sales of its biotech drug to beat its rival Amgen and its anti-anemia drugs. "The idea," as J&J drug rep Dean McClellan later explained, "was to get the docs to increase their Procrit dosage to 40,000 units."

There was just one problem. Regulators had approved a weekly drug dose of 30,000 units, and J&J was prohibited by the Food, Drug, and Cosmetic Act (FDAC) from marketing its drugs in unapproved ways. But the doctors could prescribe in any "off-label" manner they wanted. So, McClellan, a star rep and medical consigliere, led a "discussion" about high-dose

Kathleen Sharp, "Patients May Die When Doctors Moonlight as Big Pharma's 'Key Opinion Leaders,'" *Truthout.org*, January 24, 2012. First appeared at Truthout.org on January 24, 2012 at www.truth-out.org/news/item/6200:patients-may-die-when-doctors -moonlight-as-big-pharmas-key-opinion-leaders. Reprinted with permission.

experiments. Taking his cue, one physician explained how he routinely injected patients with 40,000 units of Procrit. Another oncologist pumped his people with 10,000 units for ten consecutive days—triple the approved amount. "That seems a little extreme," said McClellan, frowning.

The cancer market grew so saturated with high doses, that six years later the Food and Drug Administration finally approved them.

"Oh no," the doctor said. "I haven't seen any side effects so far."

A few months later, Procrit sales hit the $1 billion mark, beating Amgen by a hair. The resort trip had certainly helped. But it was just one part of an expansive, long-running off-label marketing campaign, according to sales documents. Slowly but surely, oncologists around the country began administering so many high Procrit doses that, in time, the off-label therapy became the "community standard."

There were problems since insurers don't always reimburse doctors for off-label use. In fact, when Medicare refused to pay the Arizona Cancer Center, a huge client, for its high-dose Procrit injections, an Ortho manager ghost wrote a letter on behalf of its chief oncologist Daniel von Hoff. After a few more company calls—*ipso presto!*—the center began receiving more than $1 million in Medicare payments for the illegal therapy. As McClellan claimed in a whistleblowing suit, the cancer market grew so saturated with high doses, that six years later the Food and Drug Administration [FDA] finally approved them.

Drug Proved to Be Unsafe

The decision might have been defensible had the 40,000-unit regime been proven to be safe and effective. But independent research later revealed that cancer patients died sooner than expected, and company trials found an alarming number of dialysis patients suffered strokes and heart attacks. Meta-studies showed that 17 percent of patients died from the drug, and stories told of blood counts so high, patients actually spit up blood and choked on their own tumors. Turns out there was little scientific evidence that Procrit, and its cousins Epogen and Aranesp, actually helped people at *any* dosage.

Last summer [2011], regulators announced that the drugs should be avoided entirely by most patients. "It turns out many people are better off taking placebos," said Dennis Cotter, president of Medical Technology and Practice Patterns, a nonprofit research institute.

What this illustrates is that drug companies can create entire cultures of over-prescribers for untested, even fatal indications, and that doctors can be easily corrupted. In light of a flurry of recent federal settlements for off-label marketing crimes, it also underlines how you, dear taxpayer, foot the bill for reckless marketing.

In the case of Procrit, the J&J unit formed advisory committees made up of academic physicians and clinical oncologists. These key opinion leaders (KOLs) were paid honoraria of at least $1,000 for every speech they delivered touting off-label use. McClellan selected some pliant clients to be the featured speakers. "Some guys wanted to give three or four speeches a weekend so they can get three or four thousand dollars," he said. A few actually did. Many talks were delivered at company "conferences" organized for other doctors, who earned hourly credits toward their annual continuing medical education (CME) units, required by state licensing boards. As if that wasn't enough, Ortho also paid physicians for their rooms, meals and transportation.

Ortho eventually assembled boards of KOLs who specialized in every type of cancer. According to sales documents, the goal was "to build thought leader endorsement [sic] to establish Procrit as standard of care," not just for approved indications such as AIDs and chemotherapy, but for cancer-related fatigue, depression, and other off-label indications.

No matter what prescribers say, they seem to have indeed been bought by golf trips, grants and banquets.

These friendly prescribers were not Dr. Feelgood types working the tenderloin. They were distinguished professors and doctors from respected institutions. . . .

One was Dr. Daniel Von Hoff, the director at the Arizona Cancer Center. He collected advisory fees and perks from not just Ortho, but from about 30 other pharmaceutical firms, earning directors' fees for sitting on several companies' boards. "When I saw how many shares he owned in biotech and drug firms, my jaw dropped," McClellan later said. Many others, like Dr. Jerome Groopman of Harvard Medical School, performed J&J-funded clinical trials. He was paid to sit on Procrit's "fatigue" advisory board and was quoted often in the *New York Times* extolling the drug, according to public records.

Groopman also penned a bestseller called *How Doctors Think*. In it, he talks about the importance of talking with patients about their diagnosis and treatments. But Groopman doesn't explain what role Big Pharma checks and trips play in his own decision making. This is noteworthy since he goes on about the influence of high-pressure drug reps and the need for physicians to weigh scientific assessments against "going with your gut."

Esteemed Doctors Were Swayed

Clearly, even esteemed doctors were swayed by Procrit's marketers. In reviewing the basic science research behind these costly anti-anemia drugs, Dr. Charles Bennett of Northwestern University found that physicians and investigators who collected money from the two drug makers were "less likely to criticize the safety, effectiveness, or cost-effectiveness of drugs" and "more likely to endorse novel and less proven treatments" like off-label. No matter what prescribers say, they seem to have indeed been bought by golf trips, grants and banquets.

The overprescribing of anti-anemia drugs roared alongside an astonishing rise in American health care expenses. For several years, Procrit and the others topped Medicare's reimbursement list. By 2007, the drugs' domestic sales approached $11 billion a year. So far, US taxpayers have shelled out more than $60 billion over the past 20 years, reimbursing doctors, KOLs and hospitals for a drug that never worked as advertised.

McClellan's whistleblowing case may be in limbo. But many prestigious doctors will soon wind up in the confessional. Thanks to the Physician Payments Sunshine Act, doctors who accept speaking fees, meals, travel, stock options, or any other compensation from drug or medical device companies will soon see their names—and their gifts—revealed publicly on the web. The rule is part of the Patient Protection and Affordable Care Act, aka "Obamacare." Data collection was supposed to begin this January [2012], but the first report won't appear until [September 2014]. When that day dawns, patients will gain some insight into their treatments. Was that off-label prescription supported by scientific evidence; or did my doctor "go with his gut?" If so, how often was that gut filled by the maker of my medication?

Proposals to Allow More Drugs to Be Sold Without a Prescription Are Controversial

Robert Goldberg

Robert Goldberg is cofounder and vice president of the Center for Medicine in the Public Interest.

Next week, the FDA [US Food and Drug Administration] will be holding a hearing about letting consumers buy commonly used prescription drugs without a prescription, signaling FDA recognition that empowering consumers to make health care choices is the key to better health at a lower cost. The agency's proposal is a refreshing departure from the usual administration's practice of expanding government's role in our daily lives. Yet so-called consumer groups that want the government to tell Americans how to eat, what cars to drive and what medicines to take are opposing even this small step toward medical freedom.

Indeed, the FDA proposal recognizes that individuals, armed with increasingly individualized information on what's best for them, can make better decisions than a system where what is spent on health care is determined by bureaucrats. More consumers want more personal responsibility and freedom in making health care decisions, not less. They want to spend less time and money on medical care. So why would some groups oppose making more medications that have been widely used for years—for such conditions as high cholesterol, migraines, and hypertension—more accessible?

Groups such as the Center for Science in the Public Interest and Public Citizen claim the FDA proposal will "permit" people to use more medicines without solid information. On the contrary, the explosion of diagnostics, applications and online communities has increased our ability to responsibly take control of our health and well-being. In today's digital world, we can use our smartphones to obtain test results and access information tailored to our diagnosis, genetics, health goals and lifestyle. Making drugs for osteoporosis prevention, birth control, migraines, cholesterol and erectile dysfunction available without a prescription would, with appropriate safeguards and new health-information tools, empower people to look after themselves. In fact, evidence shows that moving prescription drugs over the counter (OTC) helps people stay on track with their treatment regimen.

Without the ability to conveniently access and use more medicines we know and trust . . . , the paternalism of the present health care system will prevail.

Self-Care Can Improve Health

Critics often point to what they claim is misuse of cough medicines as an argument for more FDA regulation of OTC products, not less. But a recent survey I conducted on how American families treat coughs and colds underscores the opportunity self-care can offer to improve health. Over the past year, 61 million consumers avoided missing work, school or other scheduled appointments due to illness because they had access to OTC cough medicines to alleviate their symptoms. And nearly 75 percent of all consumers surveyed complemented cough and cold medicine use with rest, fluids (including chicken soup) and other "home" remedies.

The nearly a third of patients who see a physician for a cold wind up spending $7 billion on office visits and another $2 billion on antibiotics a year even though antibiotics don't work for such ailments. If we were all forced to run to the doctor and get a prescription every time we coughed or were stuffed up, we would be spending a lot more money treating symptoms that can be alleviated effectively by OTC medicines in our pharmacy or supermarket and, more often than not, resolve on their own.

So why do some groups want to keep Americans shackled to our current system of care? As [cardiologist and geneticist] Eric Topol notes in *The Creative Destruction of Medicine,* access to our "own data and information—whether it be DNA sequence or biosensor remote monitoring—will soon be unprecedented, and surely each individual has more at stake about his or her health than the busy physician who is looking after hundreds to thousands of patients . . . But change cannot take place unless consumers are the driving force." Without the ability to conveniently access and use more medicines we know and trust in tandem with such valuable personal health information, the paternalism of the present health care system will prevail. Opponents of the FDA proposal are afraid of losing control over our lives.

There is wisdom in the crowd. The benefits of consumer empowerment outweigh the risks that, in fact, can be managed mostly by we the people by educating each other. Turning more prescription medicines into OTC products not only saves time and money. It enhances our ability to sustain health rather than just treat disease.

Organizations to Contact

The editors have compiled the following list of organizations concerned with the issues debated in this book. The descriptions are derived from materials provided by the organizations. All have publications or information available for interested readers. The list was compiled on the date of publication of the present volume; names, addresses, phone and fax numbers, and e-mail and Internet addresses may change. Be aware that many organizations take several weeks or longer to respond to inquiries, so allow as much time as possible.

Alliance for the Prudent Use of Antibiotics (APUA)
200 Harrison Ave., Boston, MA   02111
(617) 636-0966 • fax: (617) 636-0458
e-mail: apua@tufts.edu
website: www.tufts.edu/med/apua

APUA's mission is to strengthen global defenses against infectious disease by ensuring access to effective treatment and promoting appropriate antibiotic use to contain drug resistance. Its website offers extensive information for consumers and doctors about the proper use of antibiotics and the danger that overuse will lead to their ineffectiveness.

Center for Public Integrity
910 17th St. NW, Suite 700, Washington, DC   20006
(202) 466-1300
website: www.publicintegrity.org

The Center for Public Integrity is a nonprofit, nonpartisan, nonadvocacy, independent journalism organization. Its mission is to serve democracy by revealing abuses of power, corruption, and betrayal of public trust by powerful public and private institutions, using the tools of investigative journalism. Its website includes a page titled "Pushing Prescriptions: How the Drug Industry Sells Its Agenda at Your Expense," which contains information about the political influence of the pharmaceutical industry.

Drug Policy Alliance (DPA)

131 W 33rd St., 15th Floor, New York, NY   10001
(212) 613-8020 • fax: (212) 613-8021
e-mail: nyc@drugpolicy.org
website: www.drugpolicy.org

DPA is a politically active organization of people who believe that the nation's present drug policy does more harm than good. Its mission is to advance those policies and attitudes that best reduce the harms of both drug use and drug prohibition, and to promote the sovereignty of individuals over their minds and bodies. Although most of its material deals with illegal drugs, its website contains many articles on prescription drug abuse and on problems related to federal drug control.

Free Medicine Foundation

PO Box 515, RR 3 Box 7833, Doniphan, MO   63935
(573) 996-3333
website: www.freemedicinefoundation.com

The Free Medicine Foundation is a nationwide patient-advocacy organization that links patients to free or very low-cost prescription plans available to eliminate or substantially reduce their prescription costs. Its website contains information about how the program works as well as comments from patients.

Healthy Skepticism

34 Methodist St., Willunga   SA 5172
   Australia
website: www.healthyskepticism.org

Healthy Skepticism is an international nonprofit organization for health professionals and everyone with an interest in improving health. Its main aim is to improve health by reducing harm from inappropriate, misleading or unethical marketing of health products or services, especially misleading pharmaceutical promotion. Its website has an extensive library of references dealing with pharmaceutical advertising and the effects it has on patterns of prescribing and medication usage.

Institute for Safe Medication Practices (ISMP)
200 Lakeside Dr., Suite 200, Horsham, PA   19044
(215) 947-7797 • fax: (215) 914-1492
website: www.ismp.org

The ISMP is the nation's only nonprofit organization devoted entirely to medication error prevention and safe medication use. Its mission is to advance patient safety worldwide by empowering the health-care community, including consumers, to prevent medication errors. It publishes four electronic *ISMP Medication Safety Alert!* newsletters and offers numerous educational tools as well as a medication error reporting program.

International Federation of Pharmaceutical
Manufacturers and Associations (IFPMA)
15 Chemin Louis-Dunant, PO Box 195, Geneva 20   1211
  Switzerland
e-mail: info@ifpma.org
website: www.ifpma.org

IFPMA is a nonprofit, nongovernmental organization representing the research-based pharmaceutical industry, with members including leading international companies as well as national and regional industry pharmaceutical associations in both developing and developed countries. It advocates policies that encourage discovery of and access to life-saving and life-enhancing medicines to improve the health of people everywhere. Its website contains its code of practice, news reports, and many downloadable publications.

National Council on Patient Information
and Education (NCPIE)
200-A Monroe St., Suite 212, Rockville, MD   20850
(301) 340-3940 • fax: (301) 340-3944

e-mail: ncpie@ncpie.info
website: www.talkaboutrx.org

The mission of NCPIE, a nonprofit coalition of close to one hundred organizations, is to stimulate and improve communication of information on appropriate medicine use to consumers and health-care professionals. It aims to ensure that medicine information is useful and scientifically accurate in whatever form and for whatever audience it is delivered. NCPIE publishes many educational resources that can be ordered, and its website contains a "Tools for Consumers" page containing useful links.

National Institute on Drug Abuse (NIDA)
Office of Science Policy and Communications
Public Information and Liaison Branch, Bethesda, MD 20892
(301) 443-1124
website: www.drugabuse.gov

NIDA's mission is to lead the nation in bringing the power of science to bear on drug abuse and addiction. Its aims are to support and conduct research, to ensure the rapid and effective dissemination and use of the results of that research to significantly improve prevention and treatment, and to inform policy as it relates to drug abuse and addiction. Its website has a section on prescription drug abuse, plus one especially for teens at http://teens.drugabuse.gov/peerx.

Partnership for Prescription Assistance (PPA)
(888) 477-1669
website: www.pparx.org

The Partnership for Prescription Assistance brings together America's pharmaceutical companies, doctors, other health-care providers, patient advocacy organizations, and community groups to help qualifying patients who lack prescription coverage get the medicines they need through the public or private program that is right for them. It offers a single point of access to more than 475 public and private programs. Its website contains information about the available programs for patients, caregivers, and doctors, plus patient testimonials.

Partnership for Safe Medicines

8100 Boone Blvd., Suite 220, Vienna, VA   22182
(703) 679-7233
website: www.safemedicines.org

Partnership for Safe Medicines is a group of nonprofit organizations and individuals that have policies, procedures, or programs to protect consumers from counterfeit or contraband medicines. Its website includes information about poisons in counterfeit medications, how to spot fakes, the risks in importing drugs, and how to buy prescription drugs safely.

Pharmaceutical Research and Manufacturers of America (PhRMA)

950 F St. NW, Suite 300, Washington, DC   20004
(202) 835-3400 • fax: (202) 835-3414
website: www.phrma.org

PhRMA represents the country's leading pharmaceutical research and biotechnology companies. Its mission is to conduct effective advocacy for public policies that encourage discovery of important new medicines. Its website contains newsletters, policy statements, fact sheets, speeches, and press releases.

PharmedOut

Georgetown University Medical Center
Dept. of Pharmacology, Washington, DC   20057
(202) 687-1191 • fax: (202) 687-8825
e-mail: nzd2@georgetown.edu
website: www.pharmedout.org

PharmedOut is a Georgetown University Medical Center project that advances evidence-based prescribing and educates health-care professionals about pharmaceutical marketing practices. Its website provides news, information, and resources including slideshows, videos, teaching tools and downloadable articles.

US Food and Drug Administration (FDA)
10903 New Hampshire Ave., Silver Spring, MD   20993
(888) 463-6332
e-mail: druginfo@fda.hhs.gov
website: www.fda.gov/drugs

The FDA is the federal agency responsible for regulating medications, including both prescription and over-the-counter drugs. Its Center for Drug Evaluation and Research (CDER) performs an essential public health task by making sure that safe and effective drugs are available to improve the health of people in the United States. Its website contains extensive information about drugs in general and official fact sheets about specific drugs.

Bibliography

Books

Otis Webb Brawley — *How We Do Harm: A Doctor Breaks Ranks About Being Sick in America.* New York: St. Martin's Press, 2012.

Peter R. Breggin — *Medication Madness.* New York: St. Martin's Press, 2009.

Shannon Brownlee — *Overtreated: Why Too Much Medicine Is Making Us Sicker and Poorer.* New York: Bloomsbury, 2008.

Rod Colvin — *Overcoming Prescription Drug Addiction.* Omaha, NE: Addicus Books, 2014.

Joseph Dumit — *Drugs for Life: How Pharmaceutical Companies Define Our Health.* Durham, NC: Duke University Press, 2012.

Carl Elliott — *White Coat, Black Hat: Adventures on the Dark Side of Medicine.* Boston, MA: Beacon Press, 2011.

Mark James Estren — *Prescription Drug Abuse.* Oakland, CA: Ronin Publishing, 2013.

Lawrence T. Friedhoff — *New Drugs: An Insider's Guide to the FDA's New Drug Approval Process for Scientists, Investors and Patients.* New York: PSPG Publishing, 2009.

Ben Goldacre — *Bad Pharma: How Drug Companies Mislead Doctors and Harm Patients.* London, United Kingdom: Faber & Faber, 2013.

Jeremy A. Greene and Elizabeth Siegel Watkins, eds. — *Prescribed: Writing, Filling, Using, and Abusing the Prescription in Modern America.* Baltimore, MD: Johns Hopkins University Press, 2012.

David Healy — *Pharmageddon.* Berkeley, CA: University of California Press, 2013.

Irving Kirsch — *The Emperor's New Drugs: Exploding the Antidepressant Myth.* New York: Basic Books, 2010.

John L. LaMattina — *Devalued and Distrusted: Can the Pharmaceutical Industry Restore its Broken Image?* Hoboken, NJ: Wiley, 2012.

Jie Jack Li — *Blockbuster Drugs: The Rise and Decline of the Pharmaceutical Industry.* New York: Oxford University Press, 2014.

Don Light, ed. — *The Risks of Prescription Drugs.* New York: Columbia University Press, 2010.

Joshua Lyon — *Pill Head: The Secret Life of a Painkiller Addict.* New York: Hyperion, 2009.

Melody Petersen — *Our Daily Meds: How the Pharmaceutical Companies Transformed Themselves into Slick Marketing Machines and Hooked the Nation on Prescription Drugs.* New York: Picador, 2009.

Marvin D. Seppala and Mark E. Rose — *Prescription Painkillers: History, Pharmacology, and Treatment.* Center City, MN: Hazelden, 2010.

Kathleen Sharp — *Blood Medicine: Blowing the Whistle on One of the Deadliest Prescription Drugs Ever.* New York: Plume, 2012.

James Soil — *Child of a Prescription Drug Abuser.* Denver, CO: Outskirts Press, 2013.

H. Gilbert Welch — *Overdiagnosed: Making People Sick in the Pursuit of Health.* Boston, MA: Beacon Press, 2011.

Robert Whitaker — *Anatomy of an Epidemic: Magic Bullets, Psychiatric Drugs, and the Astonishing Rise of Mental Illness in America.* New York: Broadway Books, 2011.

Periodicals and Internet Resources

John-Manuel Andriote — "Breaking the Cycle of Prescription Drug Costs," *The Atlantic*, October 9, 2012. www.theatlantic.com.

John-Manuel Andriote — "Legal Drug-Pushing: How Disease Mongers Keep Us All Doped Up," *The Atlantic*, April 3, 2012. www.theatlantic.com.

Patrick Arbore — "The Next Big Thing: Substance Abuse Among Aging Baby Boomers," *Aging Today*, May/June 2012. www.asaging.org.

Diane Archer — "Strengthen Medicine: End Drug Company Price Setting," Health Affairs Blog, May 28, 2013. http://healthaffairs.org.

Peter B. Bach, Leonard B. Saltz, and Robert E. Wittes — "In Cancer Care, Cost Matters," *New York Times*, October 14, 2012. www.nytimes.com.

Drake Bennett — "This Is a Fish on (Prescription) Drugs," *BusinessWeek*, February 14, 2010. www.businessweek.com.

Peter R. Breggin — "Drug Companies Drive the Psychiatric Drugging of Children," *Huffington Post*, July 24, 2012. www.huffingtonpost.com.

Monica Buchanan — "The War on Counterfeit Prescription Drugs," *NBC Connecticut*, August 15, 2013. www.nbcconnecticut.com.

Kiera Butler — "Can You Flush Your Old Drugs Down the Toilet?" *Mother Jones*, July/August 2012. www.motherjones.com.

Arthur Caplan and Zachary Caplan — "How Big Pharma Rips You Off on Drugs," *CNN Opinion*, April 25, 2013. www.cnn.com.

Allen J. Frances — "A Pill-Popping Society," *Psychology Today*, July 17, 2013. www.psychologytoday.com.

Cory Franklin — "America's Epidemic of Over-Prescribing," *The Guardian*, June 20, 2011. www.guardian.co.uk.

Brian Fung — "The $289 Billion Cost of Medication Noncompliance, and What to Do About It," *The Atlantic*, September 11, 2012. www.theatlantic.com.

W. Gifford-Jones — "Feeling Overmedicated? We've Got a Pill for That," *Winnipeg Free Press*, June 21, 2009. www.winnipegfreepress.com.

Felix Gillette — "Inside Pfizer's Fight Against Counterfeit Drugs," *BusinessWeek*, January 17, 2013. www.businessweek.com.

Paul Roderick Gregory — "Obama Care Will End Drug Advances and Europe's Free Ride (Unless China Steps In)," *Forbes*, July 1, 2012. www.forbes.com.

Matthew Herper — "The Truly Staggering Cost of Inventing New Drugs," *Forbes*, February 10, 2012. www.forbes.com.

Linda A. Johnson — "Prescription-Drug Prices to Plunge as Patents Expire," *Seattle Times*, July 24, 2011. http://seattletimes.com.

David Kroll   "The Friends You Keep: Non-Medical Use of Prescription Drugs," *Forbes*, June 20, 2013. www.forbes.com.

Marilynn Larkin   "The 'Medicalization' of Aging," *Journal on Active Aging*, January/February 2011.

Robert Lefever   "Yes, Statins Work Wonders, But I Fear We're Becoming a Nation Who'd Rather Pop Pills Than Lead Healthy Lives," *Daily Mail* (United Kingdom), August 30, 2012. www.dailymail.co.uk.

Donald W. Light   "Medicine in the Thrall of the Culture of Drugs," *Health Affairs*, December 2012. http://healthaffairs.org.

David Maris   "Who Is Popping All Those Pills?" *Forbes*, July 24, 2012. www.forbes.com.

Joey Mattingly   "Understanding Drug Pricing," *US Pharmacist*, June 20, 2012. www.uspharmacist.com.

Antonio Maturo   "Medicalization: Current Concept and Future Directions in a Bionic Society," *Mens Sana Monographs*, January 2012. www.ncbi.nlm.nih.gov.

Richard Meyer   "Prescription Drugs Take Too Much Blame for Healthcare Costs," World of DTC Marketing, April 8, 2013. http://worldofdtcmarketing.com.

National
Resources Defense
Council

"Dosed Without Prescription: Preventing Pharmaceutical Contamination of the Nation's Drinking Water," January 2010. www.nrdc.org.

Evelyn Nieves

"America's Pill-Popping Capital," *Salon*, April 11, 2012. www.salon.com.

Alice Park

"Statins Have Few Side Effects, But Should More People Be Taking Them?" *Time*, July 10, 2013. http://healthland.time.com.

Stephanie C.
Perdito

"How Safe Are the Prescription Drugs We Take? Monitoring Adverse Events and Recalls," *Searcher*, June 2012. www.infotoday.com.

Daniela Perdomo

"100,000 Americans Die Each Year from Prescription Drugs, While Pharma Companies Get Rich," *AlterNet*, June 24, 2010. www.alternet.org.

Mark Rubenstein

"Medication Nation," *Huffington Post*, May 3, 2013. www.huffingtonpost .com.

Jill Sederstrom

"Revising the NonRx Drug Category," *Drug Topics*, May 15, 2012. http://drugtopics.modernmedicine.com.

Stephanie Smith
and Nadia
Kounang

"Prescription Drugs 'Orphan' Children in Eastern Kentucky," *CNN Health*, December 14, 2012. www.cnn.com.

Mike Stobbe	"Drug Overdose Deaths Spike Among Middle-Aged Women," *The Big Story*, July 2, 2013. http://bigstory.ap.org.
Katie Thomas	"Breaking the Seal on Drug Research," *New York Times*, June 29, 2013. www.nytimes.com.
Harriet Washington	"Flacking for Big Pharma," *American Scholar*, Summer 2011. http://theamericanscholar.org.

Index

W

V

Z